CRAP TOWNS RETURNS

BACK BY UNPOPULAR DEMAND

Edited by Sam Jordison and Dan Kieran

Quercus

Thanks to everyone who wrote in to **craptownsreturns.co.uk**, or contacted us through Twitter, Facebook, and on one notable occasion, screamed about Chipping Norton in the pub. We're sorry we could only include such a small percentage of your wonderful, hilarious, joyful and furious messages.

A NOTE ON STATISTICS

The average house prices were gathered in March 2013 and will no doubt have changed already. But they give a good general idea of how things are. Expensive, aren't they?!

Average town populations were gathered from Wikipedia. Which was much easier than going through the census data, like we had to last time. At least some things have improved!

A NOTE ON THE RANKING SYSTEM

This was based on the number of nominations and recommendations flying at us through various social media platforms and craptownsreturns.com. There was a bit of weighting depending on the population of the town, the number of visits various entries received on the website and the hilarity of the nominations. It wasn't entirely scientific. But it does feel right. Even if we had to stop counting soon after High Wycombe began an extraordinary late surge and smashed into the top ten. Given another month or so, it might have hit the top spot. Maybe next time . . .

ATTRIBUTIONS

All photos taken by Sam Jordison, unless otherwise stated.

CONTENTS

Britain is crap.

It's been said before. It's been said, in fact, in the first book of Crap Towns. But when I wrote that sentence in 2003, I had no idea that it would remain so true for an entire decade. That Britain would, in fact, seem crapper than ever today.

If you'd told me back then that there would be even more absurd councils and bad planning decisions to write about, I'd have laughed even more than I was doing already. My co-editor and I were getting so many missives of woe and misery from all over the country – and so many of them were so hilariously well written – that it was hard to imagine anyone topping them. How could things get better? Or, conversely, how could Britain get even crapper?

Easily, it turned out.

Back in 2003, when the first book of Crap Towns came out, boarded-up high streets were a novelty. Youth unemployment was still sometimes regarded as a lifestyle choice instead of universal and compulsory. Riots were something that happened in history books – and not Ealing. Regeneration was a distinct possibility rather than a bitter joke. Money was flowing into previously crap towns like Hastings, Hull and Morecambe. Old buildings were being fixed up, new ones were being built – and, amazingly, they weren't all awful.

But things did not, as we were promised, only get better. Instead, the bland brand makeover continued on our high streets. Tescos appeared everywhere, killing native businesses with the steady sureness of grey squirrels destroying their cuter red cousins.

Plenty of other corporations also worked to suck the life out of our high streets and thanked us for our custom by funnelling our money into offshore tax havens. Later, when the credit crunch struck, they left those same streets lifeless and empty.

Elsewhere, the recession, the coalition and a new generation of disaffected youth and a wizened cabal of greedy old bankers made themselves equally busy writing copy for this book. In 2012 critical mass was reached. Apparently spontaneously, a 2004 article from the *Independent* about the second book of Crap Towns spent several weeks in the top ten most-read stories on independent.co.uk. Then Gary Barlow sent hundreds of thousands of followers in our direction when he tweeted about how much he'd enjoyed reading the first book of Crap Towns. At the same time, the *News and Star* in Cleator Moor started raging about the fact that their town was 'in the running' to be included in the book. Even though Cleator Moor had already appeared in Crap Towns – a full ten years ago. 'It's not that bad,' declared locals in a stirring defence.

Dan and I were yet to start thinking seriously about revisiting the project, but people were bombarding us with messages. They demanded to know when we were going to give Chipping Norton its just deserts, when we were going to reveal the truth about Banbury, why we hadn't included Great Yarmouth in the earlier versions. Nominations started flooding in.

And on that last point at least, there is cause for celebration. The worst of Britain has also brought out the best. The national talent for mockery, self-deprecation and laughing in the face of adversity remains as strong as ever. We still excel at gallows humour – and it's a good job too, because we need it more than ever . . . Which is why Crap Towns has returned: by unpopular demand.

Sam Jordison

50 SHEERNESS

Motto: Known by their fruits
Population: 13,000
Average house price: £153,000
Famous residents:
Rod Hull, Emu

In 1667, during the second Anglo-Dutch War, the Isle of Sheppey was captured by the enemy navy. It was a great victory for the Dutch, partly helped by some half-hearted resistance by the ill-fed, underpaid local garrison at Sheerness. However, after only a few days, the invaders abandoned their conquest and never returned. History regards their departure as a mystery, but common sense suggests they simply couldn't stand being in Sheerness a moment longer.

Visiting today, it is easy to sympathise with the Dutch. The town may be less than 40 miles from London, but its atmosphere of decay and abandonment makes it feel as if you have travelled to one of the less scenic industrial towns of Siberia. Surrounded by a bleak landscape of mudflats, electricity pylons and waterlogged fields, it is hard to believe that this used to be a holiday destination for working-class Londoners.

Sheerness has managed to avoid becoming a clone town, but this is only because few retailers have bothered to open branches in an area blighted by badly built housing, obese locals and a wealth of empty industrial units.

On the plus side, Sheerness does cater for some very unusual niche markets. It might be short on organic cafes and antique shops, but how many other towns provide one-stop shopping for scrap metal and sex aids?

Buff Orpington

49 BURY ST EDMUNDS

Motto: Sacrarium regis cunabula legis (Shrine of the king, cradle of the law)
Population: 33,000
Average house price: £289,000
Famous residents: Bill Wyman

The pavements are covered in wonky paving slabs. They're like that on purpose, I think, in order to look 'olde worlde', as part of the ongoing attempt to make Bury appear like its mighty cousin, Cambridge. Needless to say it's failing miserably.

The kids have nothing

to do. The adults fill their time with petty squabbles. The council and the residents spent 10 years on whether or not to build a cinema. Another 15 years were wasted working out whether or not to build more awful shops on a vast expanse of car park right in the middle of town named 'the cattle market'.

To top it all, a huge sugar beet factory looms above the skyline and every so often (normally on a lovely sunny day) emits a cloying, sickly stench over the town like a shimmering shroud of doom.

Andrew Martin

BASKET CASE
Hanging baskets were banned from Bury St Edmunds town centre after Suffolk County Council ruled there was a risk that they could fall from lampposts and injure the public.

BELL ENDS
In the 19th century the romantic novelist Ouida, who lived in Bury St Edmunds, described her home as: 'This petty-bourgeois town where the inhabitants must perforce ring their own doorbells lest they rust from disuse.'

48 OXFORD

Motto: Fortis est veritas (The truth is tough)
Population: 165,000
Average house price: £271,000
Famous residents: Just about every Tory prime minister ever, up to and including Tony Blair and David Cameron

Dreaming spires. Old mellow stones. Ornate libraries. Lovely old books. Beautiful dining halls. It's like Hogwarts for wankers.

CRAP TOWN UPDATE!
POSITION LAST TIME: 31
REASONS:
• Ghettoization of working classes into crime-ridden estates like Blackbird Leys.
• Naughty kids setting fire to bins.

We'll start with the moronity. Over a decade ago, Oxford City Council had a stroke of city planning genius: to encourage the more rowdy establishments towards a single road in the centre of town. George Street. A place where drunks can run the gamut from shitty meat-market clubs, which offer Rohypnol as part of their cheap drinks promotion, right through to Jamie Oliver's Italian restaurant for the most high-class dining imaginable to a brain untroubled by thought.

To drive down George Street on a Friday night is to recreate the experience of Windsor Safari Park with kebabs. Hairy creatures will block your way and beat their chests making loud 'oo oo oo' sounds. They will bend your aerial and display their bare bottoms. Those exhibiting less aggressive behaviour can be found in shop doorways performing acts of public copulation, sometimes shielding their faces with their overcoats. Often not.

On the other side of town sits the cultural mecca that is the Cowley Road, kind of a massive community-based hallucination of a community. You have to drink the kool-aid to be a part of it. Decades ago, Cowley Road was known as the hip, diverse and multicultural area of Oxford. In other words, it's where the poor people who had failed to get a council house with central heating lived. The squatters deluded themselves into the belief that their poverty was a bohemian experience and fabricated the mirage of a 'cultural hotpot'. If the recipe for hotpot involves lentil farts, stabbing and Prozac, then Cowley Road was, indeed, a gourmet delight. Over the years, the myth swelled to create a kind of shitty version of the Greenwich Village effect in New York. Once an area is designated 'hip', the property prices skyrocket and the vile children of moneyed families overrun it like preened rats in UGG boots.

Cowley Road has dragged its self-conscious notion of 'relevant' into yet another decade, and to walk the length of the street now is to see the worst of all human life. The big-woolly-hatted white boys with dreadlocks sipping their Costa lattes. The small gangs of youths in hologram-stickered baseball caps, who return from a trip to Brixton sucking their thumbs. Worst of all, the legions of Brookes students in their pyjamas and wife-beaters squealing with unbridled posh joy as they breathe in the atmosphere and suck out the life.

There are towns that do pretentiousness better, towns that do poverty better, towns that do mindlessness better, but as an all-rounder, I'd say Oxford's your winner. Apparently, there's also a university here . . .
Julian Frank

RECENT DEVELOPMENTS

• Oxfordshire County Council has been fighting to close libraries, including those on the deprived Blackbird Leys estate. Local residents have been fighting back. Leading the charge, local author Philip Pullman declared it 'a war against stupidity'.

• The heroic Pullman also spent years fighting developers who wanted to destroy the historic and romantic Castle Mill boatyard in the city's Jericho area. After years of struggle, the developers successfully closed the yard. Then went bust. Leaving it empty.

• Members of the Bullingdon Club, the notorious drinking society for posh people attending Oxford University, have started running the country. Into the ground.

MAYDAY! MAYDAY!

47 GLASTONBURY

Motto: Floreat ecclesia angliae (May the Anglican Church prosper)
Population: 32,000
Average house price: £260,000
Famous residents: King Arthur, Jesus Christ, Sally Morningstar (hedgewitch, author of 26 books)

Most famous for the nearby festival, the town of Glastonbury also attracts tourists in its own right, thanks to its ancient tor, attractive old buildings and a limitless supply of ageing hippies in rainbow-coloured jumpers.

If you ask most locals, they'll tell you that Glastonbury is one of the most beautiful, most colourful and most spiritual places in the entire nation.

But then, if you ask most locals, they will also tell you that water has a memory, and that vibrating it with infinitely minute quantities of various poisons will produce a drink that cures any disease – so long as the patient parts with enough money before swallowing.

Residents are also likely to tell you that we're about to be visited by benevolent beings from the world of infinite light. And that in the next few days they intend to dance wildly, meditate deeply and frolic abundantly, barefoot in a field.

Then they will try to hold your hand and tell you about Wicca.

They will encroach on your comfort zone. They will tell you they knew Hendrix and that they used to get high simply by listening to his music. They will tell you that they were taught about tantric sex in a temple in the Himalayas. They will tell you that those were wild times and roll their eyes and touch your leg and they won't move their hand away, even when you pull back.

They will have thinning hair and a ponytail. They will smell of patchouli and weed and lonely, angry wanking. They will wear sandals in winter. They will tell you that they have in their possession certain oils, extracted from certain plant essences that really aren't too expensive,

considering their health-giving properties, should you choose to buy some, which you really should. They will ogle your breasts and try to sell you a dream catcher. Or a crystal that will ward off cancer and that 'really sets off your sensual eyes'.

They will put on whale music. They will tell you that you look stressed and that they know the cure. They will say that this cure was passed down to them by ancient masters and that they have healing hands. They will say you look like you need a massage. They will say that even Indian gurus normally pay them, so don't look so shocked at the price. They will say that, yes, you do have to be naked before they can perform the massage – and that they do too. Then they will start to take off their clothes . . .

. . . It's time to leave.

Jane Asherton

MOVING

My friend moved to Glastonbury and changed his name to Robin Rainbow Warrior Hood.
Caroline

GRAIL QUEST

According to legend, King Arthur once reigned in Glastonbury. In fact, the town lies on the ancient island of Avalon! And Arthur was buried there alongside his lady love Guinevere.

Glastonbury is also at the centre and convergence of a number of important ley lines. Some say this is perhaps why Joseph of Arimathea travelled there carrying a cup of Jesus Christ's blood, also known as the Holy Grail. They also say Joseph travelled to Glastonbury by boat, floating across the flooded Somerset Levels. On disembarking, he struck the ground with his staff – and in that place there flowered the Glastonbury Thorn. Even now, there is a certain hawthorn tree that only grows within a few miles of Glastonbury, and which flowers twice of a year: once in spring and again around Christmas time.[1]

[1] None of this shit is true.

Photos (except tower): Caroline

RHYL

**Motto: Yr hafan deg ar fin y don (The fair haven at the edge of the waves)
Population: 60,000
Average house price: £144,000
Famous residents: Ruth Ellis (the last woman to be hanged in the UK), Lee Evans (comedian), Peter Moore (serial killer)**

The last time Rhyl made the news was when John Prescott punched a man in the face there, and its most famous daughter is Ruth Ellis, the last British woman to be hanged. But there's more to the town than violence. There's lots of concrete too.

I hit Rhyl on the home straight of a long tour of Shit Britain. By that stage I was feeling pretty much immune to blight and decay, along with hypothermia, e. coli and WKD Blue. I'd even primed myself with two nights at Pontin's Southport, entertained by Keith Harris and Orville and drunk children throwing up into the snow-dusted fag bins. But Rhyl was something else. There's nowhere grimmer than a town that was purpose-built for having a good time, and is now having a very bad one – particularly in February. Failing to rise to the twin challenges of its bleak, silly name and being on Liverpool Bay, Rhyl has skulked away into the shadowy overlap that exists between the melancholy of a faded seaside resort and the heavier shit of hardcore urban degeneration.

The ranks of weathered white oblongs gave Rhyl's outlying static-caravan belt the look of a neglected war cemetery. In the unpeopled streets beyond them, the only spark of life was a price war being fought out amongst takeaways (CHEAPEST CHIPS IN RHYL) and pound shops (EVERYTHING NOW 98p). Most of the hefty old guesthouses on the sea front were boarded up or burnt out. Those that weren't, I'd been told, are now occupied by rehoused Liverpudlian opiate enthusiasts, though I thought better of confirming this with a door-to-door survey. (Rhyl became Smackhead-on-Sea thanks to a 14-year-old

Mr Big, who kept his stash in those plastic capsules out of Kinder Eggs and was driven around in a limo by two heavies: it sounds like Junior Apprentice for class-A drug dealers.)

The one thing almost worth looking at – the deep brown sea – had been hidden from view by a massive concrete wall. Most of the streets leading away from it appeared to have been cluster-bombed. Courtesy of a predictably catastrophic 70s makeover, the Edwardian pier and theatre had given way to a gigantic corrugated shed that would soon be hosting Go West – the 25th Anniversary Tour, and exuded all the ritzy, vibrant appeal of a Chernobyl bus depot. The weathered plastic barn beside it was the Rhyl Sun Centre, opened to great fanfare in 1980, but now less like a climate-controlled aquatic paradise than somewhere you might find yourself losing an argument

CRAP TOWNS TRIVIA

TO HULL AND BACK

Being crap isn't the only thing that Rhyl has in common with Hull. Until the 16th century, the town was known as Hull. It changed to Hyll some time around 1600 – Rhil around 1700 and Rhyl in 1840. Some people also say that the name Rhyl originates from the Welsh 'Ty yn yr haul' meaning 'House in the sun'. Those people don't know much about the weather in Rhyl.

with customer services about a faulty leaf blower.

Rhyl's core customers must have been pretty difficult to alienate: they were from Wolverhampton. You have to salute the tireless dedication with which Rhyl's elders have made their once lovely and popular town so impressively unlikeable. From residents to erstwhile holidaymakers, it's now almost impossible to find anyone with a good word to say about the place. 'My aunt is the mayor of Rhyl,' began my favourite onslaught, 'but family loyalty aside, it's the most awful place I know.' *Tim Moore*[2]

[2] Tim Moore undertook this tour to write his book *You Are Awful (But I Like You): Travels Through Unloved Britain.* Crap Fans will love it.

45 BLACKBURN

**Motto: Arte et labore (By craft and labour)
Population: 105,000
Average house price: £142,000
Famous residents:** 4,000 holes, Russell Harty, Ian McShane

Twinned with Péronne, a war-ravaged part of the Somme region, Blackburn has a similar post-devastation chic. Empty streets, shuttered shop-fronts and dour-faced social anomalies permeate the town.

Around 25 per cent of the population are Muslim and, if my experiences stand for anything, the other 75 per cent appear to be aggressive racists. While enjoying a watery pint of Murphy's in an Irish pub (one of four open drinking holes) I was treated to a pensioner shouting at his own football team on the television – because there were too many 'fucking foreigners' playing organised team sport. Obviously. Talking of televisions, a local man was recently arrested for stealing his friend's TV whilst said friend was busy showering.

Last year 3,406 people suffered violence or wounding in Blackburn alone, making GBH just about the only hobby on offer.
Rory Hill

[BAD COUNCIL]

WHOLLY HOLY
The famous reference to Blackburn in the Beatles song 'A Day in the Life' came from an article John and Paul spotted in the *Daily Mail* on 17 January 1967. It explained that a local council survey had discovered that there were 4,000 potholes in the town's roads – 'one twenty-sixth' of a hole per person in Blackburn. The report cost so much to commission that the council was unable to afford to repair a single one of the 4,000 holes.

44 BOSTON

Motto: Serve with amity
Population: 36,000
Average house price: £190,000
Famous residents: Biff Byford (lead singer of Saxon), Old Mother Riley

Until the 17th century, Boston was one of Britain's most important towns. Then everyone left and it became one of the most boring instead.

Boston, or 'not that Boston, the other one', as we locals have to describe it, has been in a steady state of decline since at least the 17th century. It was then that a third of the town's population decided they could no longer stand the flat fenland landscape and set off across the Atlantic Ocean. They travelled to America in wooden boats to found what they tellingly described as 'a city on the hill'. This place, of course, was the more famous Boston, Massachusetts, and we've been living in its shadow ever since.

But although the town's fortunes have declined, there has been no accompanying belt-tightening. Boston's main claim to fame used to be that it had the highest proportion of obese people per capita in the UK until Gateshead and its burger shops usurped its (reinforced) throne.

There is still one chart we top. Boston has the highest percentage of recent immigrants in the UK. This has caused problems. Although

CRAP TOWNS TRIVIA

A MOVING STORY
In 2007 the single-issue Boston Bypass Independents won 25 out of 32 seats on the local council. Their slogan was 'Getting Boston Moving' – which they intended to do by building a road around the town. The new council leader Richard Austin said that his party's victory was: 'only a reflection of this black mood of the people of Boston . . . they really do want something to happen to Boston that isn't happening at the moment.' It still isn't happening. The road is yet to be built. The party has since been defeated.

our Bostonian ancestors thought nothing of taking over great swathes of America, banishing the local population to reservations and forcing them to work in casinos, our own attitude to incomers has been less than welcoming. Race riots broke out in the town in 2004 and 2006 following English football defeats. Windows of Portuguese and Eastern European bars and shops were smashed, police cars were overturned, petrol bombs thrown. It almost got exciting – but since then life has returned to the steady thrum of disillusionment, disappointment and resentment and too many people voting for the BNP.

The only thing that still surprises me about the place is that only a third of the population left for America. And that I didn't leave long ago too.

William Blaxton

SKEGGY

Boston is frequently described as an 'historic market town'. And it does have a market. If you like knocked-off DVDs and hideous clothes of dubious origin, you won't even be disappointed. Otherwise, you're better off going to Skegness. Which is not something you can say about anywhere else.

Mark Neal

NO JOKE

In a letter to Groucho Marx, Fred Allen wrote: 'I have just returned from Boston. It is the only sane thing to do if you find yourself up there.' That's right. Even the best and most appropriate joke for our town is actually about the place in America.

Charlie Chaplin

CRAP TOWNS TRIVIA

BOSTON UTD FOOTBALL CLUB, A TIMELINE

1932–3 The club first enters financial liquidation.

1964 Financial problems force the club to take on amateur status.

1967 Now on a more secure financial footing, the club try to rejoin the Midland League. They are refused entry.

1977 Boston are playing well! They look likely to gain promotion to the Football League – but are refused entry at the last minute because their ground is too much of a mess.

2001 Finally promoted to the Football League. Almost immediately, manager Steve Evans and a former club chairman Pat Malkinson are charged with breaking FA rules on player registration. Both men receive bans. The club is fined £100,000 and docked four points.

2007 Boston Utd FC – again – enters financial administration and is relegated to the Northern Premier league.

2007 The club also lose their entire squad but for two players.

2011 The club's joint managers, Rob Scott and Paul Hurst, resign and join local rivals Grimsby. The chairman starts legal proceedings against them.

43 FOUR MARKS

Population: 4,000
Average house price: £377,000

The town in Britain whose name most neatly corresponds to what it gets out of ten.
Dan

Four Marks photo: D. Etherington

42 NEWQUAY

Population: 20,000
Average house price: £238,000
Famous residents: William Golding (author of *Lord of The Flies*), Philip Schofield

William Golding was born in Newquay. Then he wrote a famous book about kids turning savage and torturing each other. These are not coincidences.

Once a fairly standard seaside town, populated by fishermen and laid-back surfers, Newquay has now been turned into a southern Blackpool or a British Ibiza.

During the winter, the weather coming in off the Atlantic turns the town grey, and the lack of tourists causes half the shops to shut down. The jobs available, tedious at the best of times, disappear until the summer.

And when the summer arrives, it gets worse. On hot days hung-over meatheads walk around topless in a competition to decide who uses the best steroids and the worst tattooist, hooting like apes at the occasional passing blonde. If it rains, the beaches evacuate and the tiny high street fills to bursting point.

Parents try to keep their children entertained but as every other shop only sells 'Newquay Lifeguard' hoodies, they are fighting a losing battle.

The odd couple of pensioners dodge fearfully through herds of school leavers who think the *Inbetweeners* movie is a documentary . . . But the worst is yet to come.

It's wise for anyone over 25 to get off the streets before night falls. Every beer garden fills with stag parties in matching polo shirts. Groups of cackling hens, always dressed as cowgirls, outnumbered at least five to one, attract men like the proverbial flies on doggy-do. Despite the number of bars and clubs the groups funnel through town and end up packed to the rafters in Sailors night club until it's time for a kebab and a fight.

Then, in these post-kebab small hours, Newquay recalls the fall of Rome. Couples make the most of the time they have left, before they sober up and the beer-goggles come off. In the street. In the bushes. On one notable occasion, in a skip. Less fortunate lads walk girls back to the Travelodge and are left at the door, clawing at the windows, like extras from *Day of the Dead*.

They say tourism is our major industry but this is something different, it is hedonism as imagined by Henry Ford – a conveyor belt filled with Britain's youngsters, force-fed organised fun and ironically named shots and dropping off at the other end with the thousand-yard stare of a Vietnam veteran.

Ben

CRAP TOWNS TRIVIA

THE BIRDS

In March 2013 the *Cornish Guardian* ran the astonishing headline: 'Horrified Children Watch As Seagulls Swoop On Ducklings'. Thanks to budget cuts, the town has been unable to fight off predatory seagulls this year, and the local duck population has fallen by 80 per cent. During one harrowing attack, the fluffy little yellow baby birds were snatched up in front of children in local parks.

41 HATFIELD

Population: 30,000
Average house price: £267,000
Famous residents: Dale Winton, Norman Wisdom, Barbara Cartland

It's known locally as Shatfield – although that nickname almost certainly exaggerates the town's attractions. A brown field would be quite

nice compared to the actual town, where every other house looks like a German war bunker. Except less clean and spacious on the inside.

The majority of these bomb shelters are rented to students, since nobody would want to live there long-term. So, rubbish does not make it to the dump between tenants. Dirty bedding, beer cans and planks of wood are left on the street or in front gardens. Mould spores have also been fashionable in Hatfield bathrooms for many years now. But if student homes aren't your thing, it gets worse: the two high-rise apartment block monstrosities that erupt out of the already ugly town centre like the heads of a hydra.

Also, walking in Hatfield is generally frowned upon, due to the recent popularity of mugging, rapes and bottling people outside the Town Inn. Furthermore, the only nightclub is closed throughout most of the summer, and the only building of historical interest closed throughout the winter. Oddly, however, an ice-cream van is available all year round, playing its nails-on-blackboard chime late into the night.

Future developments include an incinerator on the outskirts of town, to drown out the smell of piss with the smell of burning rubbish.

Charlotte

Hatfield photo: Jon Block

㊵ WORKSOP

Motto: Sans dieu rien (A godless nothing)
Population: 40,000
Average house price: £154,000
Famous residents: Bruce Dickinson (lead singer of Iron Maiden)

Worksop calls itself 'The Gateway to the Dukeries'. We're not sure what that means either. It used to be a mining town, but all that remains from its industrial past is emphysema.

Worksop can be most aptly summed up by a recommendation given to me by one of the locals. He informed me that the best thing to do on a Thursday night would be to head down to the local 'Witherspoons' (apparently it has an 'i' in it in these parts) as there I would

be able to see 'lots of fights'.

Here is a town with nothing to recommend it. No restaurant food other than what can be served in pubs or taken home in styrofoam, very little to do or of cultural interest. Even Starbucks have so far avoided the place.[3]

And what is Worksop most famous for? Why, it was named the heroin capital of Europe. In 2004, it was revealed that there were more than 1,200 heroin addicts in the area, affecting one in three households in the town.

'M'

NEIGHBOURLY

I lived in Manton in Worksop for a year. My windows were bricked up. I was burgled. Someone graffitied my door. Oh, and I was threatened with a knife.

[3] Since this entry was sent into craptownsreturns.com, a Starbucks has in fact opened in the town. But that shouldn't necessarily be seen as an improvement

Huntingdon photo: Lorna Hughes

㊴ HUNTINGDON

Motto: A special kind of place
Population: 20,000
Average house price: £198,000
Famous residents: Oliver Cromwell,
John Major, Sid Owen

The cover star of *Crap Towns II* thanks to its remarkably ugly town centre, Huntingdon continues to attract opprobrium. And exploding pigeons . . .

Before it appeared on the front cover of *Crap Towns II*, the nation's awareness of Huntingdon was entirely based on it being home to two of the greyest, most conservative leaders in British history: Oliver Cromwell, who famously outlawed Christmas, and John Major, a Prime Minister with all the charisma of a washing powder tablet.

With heroes like that, it's no wonder that Huntingdon finds itself wrapped up in a blanket of tedium, shaking an angry fist at the winds of change. The town has been represented by a Conservative MP for over 80 unbroken years. Even in 2001, when Tory candidates elsewhere were losing to decorative fruit baskets and waxworks of the late Peter Cook,

silly-named Jonathan Djanogly still bagged 50 per cent of the vote. Whatever your personal politics may be, that sustained level of commitment to avoiding change suggests a certain lack of imagination.

Although the town boasts occasional high points – Britain's largest meadow lies on its outskirts, for example – these only manage to briefly punctuate the monotony, like the commas in a passage of European fishing quota legislation.

Even the Huntingdon Life Sciences protesters got bored and left some years ago,

presumably reasoning that releasing the animals from the lab into the town would in fact be less humane than keeping them caged.
Snotty [4]

RECENT DEVELOPMENTS

• A village near Huntingdon was bombarded with burning pigeons in early 2013. So many of the rat-birds sat on the top wire of an overhead cable that they caused the wire they were on to touch the wire below. This sparked a huge explosion and sent them hurtling into the sky, consumed by flames.

• Less amusingly, a charity discovered 31 per cent of children in the Huntingdon North district live in poverty.

[4] You can read more from Snotty at: http://landofdopeandtories.wordpress.com/

38 BURNHAM MARKET

Population: 948
Average house price: £494,000
Famous residents: Amanda Holden

Dubbed Chelsea-On-Sea thanks to all the Londoners who have moved there, and who flock around posh hotel The Hoste Arms.

Burnham Market is serene at 5am, just as the sun is rising. It's also quite fun around 8am when the sweet old locals scurry about doing their shopping. But after that, people who can only communicate by shouting and braying fill the streets. They drown out all other sounds except the roar of over-expensive engines. It has the noise and the charm of a donkey farm.
Sharon

CRAP TOWNS TRIVIA

A LOAD OF COCKS

The town made the headlines in 2010 when a group of London incomers took legal action because cockerels on nearby allotments were waking them up in the morning.

37 JARROW

Population: 28,000
Average house price: £111,000
Famous residents: Catherine Cookson

In the 1930s Jarrow symbolised all that was wrong in the Great Depression. It could probably serve a similar function today – if only anyone cared enough about the place.

The only thing most people know about Jarrow is that in 1936 the town's unemployed marched to London to protest about the lack of jobs here. Nothing memorable has happened since – unless you also count the 1939 publication of local MP Ellen Wilkinson's book, *The Town That Was Murdered*. If she were writing it today, she'd have had to call it *The Town*

That Was Murdered And Whose Corpse Was Kicked. Hard. For Seventy Years.

Although, thinking about it, if she were around now, like plenty of other folk round these parts, she probably wouldn't have gone to the effort.

Charlie Palmer

[BAD COUNCIL]

MONKEY BUSINESS

Between 2008 and 2009, residents in the South Tyneside borough were kept amused by a blog from one Mr Monkey. It asked questions like 'Is the Member for Jarrow a Peckish Plonker?', posted useful advice such as 'How to recognise a coke-head' and ran a popular regular feature about the local councillors under the banner 'twat of the week'. Mr Monkey also exposed stories of ballot rigging, electoral fraud and corruption. Which perhaps explains why the council hired an American law firm and spent three years trying to unmask Mr Monkey.

In October 2012 a Freedom of Information request revealed that the council had so far spent £142,725 trying to discover the blog author's identity. They then also embarked on further legal proceedings against a member of their own council, Ahmed Khan, who had himself launched a legal challenge to stop the council spending any more money chasing the elusive Mr Monkey. Khan predicted that action would cost yet another fortune.

The identity of Mr Monkey remained undiscovered. During the same three-year period, local libraries had £250,000 cut from their budgets, leading to reduced opening hours.

36 TILSTON

Population: 627
Average house price: £674,000
Famous residents: None

A backwater whose sole purpose seems to be to perpetuate every backward village stereotype, Tilston is separated from the main road to the north and from the Welsh border to the south by several miles – and from the present day by at least a century.

This two-pub, one-shop agricultural throwback has little going for it other than as an example of the weird dichotomy that exists in isolated rural areas when overpaid bankers buy old farm houses and refit them at exorbitant cost and then attempt to co-exist with the local people – some of whom still point at the sky when planes fly over.

And then there's the hunt: proof that residing in the restricted upper echelons of the gene pool is no barrier to balancing on a horse while pissed out of your head.

Once, I approached a hunt riding near Tilston and asked why they killed fox cubs. I was told by a particularly waspish Hooray Henrietta that: 'It removes the weak cubs from the pack.'

'Isn't the point that you're controlling fox numbers?' I replied. 'Haven't you ever heard of Charles Darwin?'

It's been years, she's still trying to figure it out. Meanwhile, Tilston runs along like some weird *Archers* parody; all angry farmers, corrupt jockeys, mad gardeners, and the steady retreat into alcoholism.

Darren Straker

CRAP TOWNS TRIVIA The 2011 parish plan for Tilston states that, between 2005 and 2011, 66 residents of the village were victims of anti-social behaviour; 42 suffered vandalism. Meanwhile, 14 per cent of the total population had been burgled. Overall, a whopping 43 per cent of respondents said they had experienced crime. So much for *The Archers*. It's more like *The Wire*.

③⑤ ANTRIM

Motto: Per angusta ad augusta (Through hard times to a town in Maine, USA)
Population: 20,000
Average house price: £164,000
Famous residents: Alexander Irvine

County Antrim is beautiful. Antrim the town isn't bad either. But that shouldn't encourage you to visit . . . If you value your life

PIGS IN CRAP

Antrim's most famous former resident, Alexander Irvine, was a poet who wrote a book called *My Lady Of The Chimney Corner* (the odd title being a reference to his mother). Antrim features as a 'a purty good place fur pigs an' sich to live in'.

CRAP TOWNS TRIVIA

FOR REAL

Anyone wanting a look at the 'real' Ireland should run through Antrim. Dilapidated council estates, more sportswear than Niketown Oxford Circus and 12-year-old girls scary enough to make you want your mummy.

It has, admittedly, enjoyed a clean up, but having lived there for nine years I can vouch for the fact that it is, on the whole, a dangerous shitpit.
John Laverty

CLOCKING OFF

I quite liked Antrim when I first visited. There was a pretty old tower, an enjoyably weird masonic hall and an attractive river. But I was told to book a taxi if I wanted to go anywhere after 10pm – 'for your own safety'. Then I was told, 'actually, with your accent, just stay inside.'
'George Best'

34 GATESHEAD

**Motto: Caput inter nubila condit (The head hides among the clouds)
Population: 79,000
Average house price: £168,000
Famous residents: Marcus Bentley** (narrator of *Big Brother*), **Paul Gascoigne, Chris Waddle**

Lying on the south bank of the river Tyne, Gateshead has no fewer than seven bridges to Newcastle. Apparently, the locals have planned their escape very carefully.

In 1934 JB Priestley observed that Gateshead appeared to have been designed by an enemy of the human race. He said no real civilization could have produced 'such a town' and that it was 'nothing better' than a huge and dingy 'dormitory'.

In 2013, of course, we look back on 1934 as a better era. Fair enough, it was pretty bad when Priestley visited during the Great Depression. Hence the name. All those factory closures were tragedies, right enough. But at least people then had jobs to lose. When the current recession came around we barely noticed. After all, it's hard to go down when you're already on the floor.

Just consider: in 2007, when everyone else was enjoying the late stages of the New Labour boom, the Newcastle *Evening Chronicle* gleefully reported: 'Bulldozers are due to start the demolition of Gateshead town centre today.' That's how bad it had got. Most of the centre actually consisted of the (then) worst building in the UK, the brutal giant Trinity Centre car park and shopping centre – better known as the Get Carter Park. It had a starring role in the Michael Caine film as the fucking ugly place from the top of which Caine threw the corrupt local businessman Cliff Brumby. It was chosen by the filmmakers because it was falling down and awful back in 1971. But it lingered on another 40 years,

FAT CITY

In 2011 Gateshead was named as Britain's fat capital, sharing with Tamworth the distinction of having a higher percentage of obese people than anywhere else in the UK. Danny Dorling, a professor of human geography at Sheffield University, described Gateshead as an 'obesogenic environment' – meaning there are shed loads of fast food outlets and few open spaces for exercise.

IN DENIAL

In January 2007 a woman was denied a tourist visa to the UK because she made the mistake of telling immigration officials that she wanted to spend a week on holiday in Gateshead. They ruled that this was 'not credible'.

NO?

mouldering, rotting, stinking up the skyline, symbolizing our decline. Some people even came to quite like it.

And now it's gone (the remains sold off in commemorative tins for £5 each), you'd think we might be pleased. But what have they put up in place of this massive folly? How have they learned from the mistakes of the past? To what end have the powers that be in Gateshead used this golden opportunity to regenerate the centre and do something new and interesting for the town? That's right. They've built another car park and mall.

The only difference is that this time the great ugly box is dominated by a gigantic Tesco – just to ensure that the last few locally owned businesses are driven even deeper into the ground. Clearly, the enemies of the human race are still pushing all the buttons round here.
Kathy Armstrong

Pretty much the first thing I saw when I arrived in Gateshead was a spaced-out woman walk out into the road in front of a bus.

'Watch out, Mam, man, ya divvy,' yelled her son and pulled her back to the curb. 'You almost got run over.'

'It's lethal round here, man,' she said. 'And mind your swearing too.'

She was right about the roads. They were chaos: a weird combination of snarled up and simultaneously dangerously fast-moving traffic. There were holes and barriers and workmen everywhere, causing queues and stoppages and sudden bursts of frantic speed.

Almost the entire city centre was being renewed – but not in a good way. Behind tall metal fences, a huge new building was going up. One which seemed to have maintained most of the vices of the huge old building it was replacing, without its sole virtue of being interesting. This thing was gigantic, shapeless, corporate and completely bland. They were actually making Gateshead worse.

I was hungry. But when I saw the state of the people rolling out of the nearest pub (the only place in the centre to get a sit-down dinner that I saw), I decided it might be safer to try a baker. Inside, I saw one sandwich, 50 pies and two slabs of doughy grease that a sign told me were 'stotties'. I took the sandwich.

Back on the street, a man with no teeth was pulling a woman along by her hair while a crowd of street drinkers urged him on. Unexpectedly, she was laughing.

I ate my sandwich. It was horrible. Horns beeped. Women shouted at their children. Men shouted at each other. A glass smashed. Pneumatic drills tore at the roads. A man with a clipboard asked me for money and started following me along the street, staring and stamping his feet.

After a few hours in Gateshead I was starting to feel that getting run over by a bus would come as light relief.

Sam

FLY, YOU FOOLS!

33 BROXBURN

**Population: 13,000
Average house
price: £150,000
Famous residents:
George Clooney
once visited a local**
**(disused) lunatic asylum
while scouting for film
locations**

Broxburn is one of the
Scottish Central Belt's many
forgotten small towns.
Forgotten by those who don't
have the misfortune to live
there, anyway.

SCARRED FOR LIFE

Slumbering malevolently
beneath one of the many
industrial slag heaps that
scar the area, Broxburn's
main distinguishing features
are religious bigotry,
alcoholism, drug guzzling
(previously solvents and
lighter fluid, now cannabis
and ecstasy), Sixties housing
schemes and hopelessness. The loss of the
major local industries (car manufacture, steel,
mining, others too numerous to mention) and
their replacement by jobs at the low end of
the service/electronics industries tore the
heart out of the town. And the soul. And the
gonads.

The town's social life – which was badly
hit by the closure of the last remaining public
toilet in 1991 – is mainly concerned with
fighting, drinking, smoking dope and hanging
around the main street from 8pm onwards.
There the distractions include frightening
little old ladies, shouting abuse at women
on their own, being sick into litter bins and,
occasionally, being picked up by the police.
Ross McBurnie

POETRY

Football
addicted
bigoted
grey
wet
cold
post
industrial
unemployment
nightmare.
Graham Macindoe

㉜ LOUTH

**Motto: Deo adjuvante non timendum
(With God's help, don't be scared)
Population: 16,000
Average house price: £190,000
Famous residents: Jeffrey Archer
(disgraced Conservative peer), Roy
Chubby Brown (disgraceful comedian)**

Louth is a pleasant, quiet little town. And yes, that is a nice way of saying it's as dull as a sermon, but gentleness really is nothing to hold against the place. You could even probably admire the way the local high street has held out against the bland chain store makeover, still has a local identity and still doesn't have a McDonald's.

But Louth has a dark heart. It is the centre of a lurking and terrible evil. And no, I'm not talking about the insidious activities of the many local masons. I'm talking about something far worse. Louth is the headquarters of the British Sprout Growers Association; a body devoted to a food that looks like mini green brains, tastes like an even worse kind of cabbage and makes you fart like a dying dog. And if that isn't a reason to condemn it, I don't know what is.

Richard Cookson

㉛ NEWTON STEWART

**Population: 4,000
Average house
price: £156,000
Famous residents:
Bill Drummond
from the KLF**

Known to those desperate to escape as Mutant Stewart, the town is otherwise most famous for being one of the primary locations for the original version of *The Wicker Man* – and because, while filming, Britt Ekland described the place as: 'The town that God forgot'.

The movie required a cast of deranged-looking locals capable of being taken for pagan-worshipping bobby-barbecuing bastards. Living here you realize it was more documentary than fiction.

Oscar Apfel

30 WARRINGTON

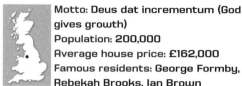

Motto: Deus dat incrementum (God gives growth)
Population: 200,000
Average house price: £162,000
Famous residents: George Formby, Rebekah Brooks, Ian Brown

Warrington is characterised by lots of angry men all produced from the same mould. Think of the thick-set, no-necked Neanderthal type from all those 'development of early man' charts you see on biology/history class walls. Then add a Warrington Wolves rugby league shirt, a couple of tattoos, and a shaved head.

Outsiders attain a kind of novelty status. They get the same kind of reception Western explorers received when they first encountered tribes in Africa and the Amazon. Here, Cosmopolitan is just a magazine.

The major landmark of the area is the Lever Brothers factory in the centre of town. This ugly monolith makes the place smell of washing powder . . . Insert your own hygiene/ irony joke – and be assured that it's probably true.

Gary Dutton

THE DEVIL'S WORK

A woman in a pub called the Lower Angel once sat next to me, stroked my leg and told me the soul of her dead husband guided her through the jewelled ring she wore. She called it the eye of the tiger. She was about 80.

Same night, a pair sitting next to us had just bumped into each other for the first time in two decades. They had been next-door neighbours. They had a good catch-up. I eavesdropped. After several chucklesome anecdotes, one confessed he once dug through the wall of the other, burgled him, and then repaired the wall. He thought it was hilarious – he could laugh about stuff like that now he was out of prison. The other guy went quiet. I thought there'd be a fight. Finally he said: 'That was you? You cheeky bugger. We never figured out where the telly went.'

Warrington is the only part of this corrupt country with any dignity left.

Alastair Harper

29 MERTHYR TYDFIL

Motto: Nid cadarn nnd brodyrdde (No strength but in fellowship)
Population: 56,000
Average house price: £132,000
Famous residents: Laura Ashley, Keir Hardie

The bleakly beautiful Brecon Beacons sweep majestically south, and come to a jarring, splattering halt in Merthyr Tydfil.

Sprawling housing estates, decaying warehouses, empty shops. Park up a few tanks, and it could be East Germany before the Berlin Wall came down.

The saddest thing is that it was once an industrial powerhouse and a hotbed of radical politics, but it has long since had the life sucked from it. Now most people resemble morlocks, only with bluer skin, and fewer aspirations. 'Merthyr is as good as any place I've been to,' they will tell you as they gorge on the three key food groups – beer, chips and 20 Bensons.

I grew up in Merthyr. I moved aged 18. I started packing my bags at 16.
Anon

CRAP TOWNS TRIVIA

ABANDON HOPE
In 1939 a report by the Political and Economic Planning think-tank recommended that Merthyr be abandoned as a hopeless case. They claimed that it did not seem reasonable 'to ask the tax-payers of the rest of Britain indefinitely to pay hundreds of thousands of pounds a year in order to give large numbers of people the dubious pleasure and benefit of continuing to live at subsistence level' in the town. And that was before Thatcher, when things started to get really bad . . .

28 BLACKPOOL

Motto: Progress
Population: 140,000
Average house
price: £108,000
Famous residents:
Ken Dodd, Frank
Carson, Peter Purves

Blackpool tries to give people a good time. They show their gratitude by fighting and puking in the streets.

I went to Blackpool once. It was like walking through a Hieronymus Bosch painting. Hordes of topless folk hung out of pub windows, yelling, drooling, puking, pissed. Out on the streets there was shouting, fighting, bum-showing and bottle-throwing – and that was just the ladies on hen-dos. Their male counterparts were mainly passed out in their own bodily fluids – even though it was only three o'clock in the

afternoon. I wouldn't have been surprised to see imps with pitchforks come along and start loading them onto carts . . . But what I actually saw was a woman wearing 'L' plates trying to touch a donkey's privates.

It was then that I decided to go home.

Blackpool is all the proof I need that God doesn't exist. If He were looking, He would have burned the place.

Miles Cross

BLACKPOOL DEFENDED!

Blackpool is one of my favourite colours. Greige – the colour of old hearing-aids and filing cabinets. Beautiful!

My favourite arcade in Blackpool sells cups of tea for 10p. With each cup you get a free Gamblers Anonymous leaflet. I paid for my tea in 2p coins (that I'd won from the pushers) and the tea-man didn't bat an eyelid.

Jenn Ashworth

BLACKPOOL DEFENDED AGAIN! KIND OF!

Apparently Blackpool has the greatest proportion of single male homeless divorcees in its population than any other town or city in Britain. When you've lost your wife, lost your job, and lost your house, there's always Blackpool.

Jamie Ashmore

LIFE'S A BEACH
In summer 2012 the Marine Conservation Society warned that holidaymakers would stop visiting Blackpool if they realised the local sea water is still dirty.

'A big issue in the North West is wrongly connected toilets and washing machines which are plumbed into the wrong waste pipes,' said Dr Robert Keirle. 'If visitors are aware that the water quality is still poor they are going to vote with their feet and go to the next resort where the water is cleaner.'

To prove his point, that same summer, the sea around the Blackpool coast briefly turned orange.[5]

[5] Thanks to an influx of Noctiluca algae, which is apparently harmless, even if it makes the sea look like J20.

HAPLESS

In a show of honesty rare among politicians, Blackpool's Labour council leader recently published a letter admitting that Blackpool has become a 'refuge of the dispossessed' and 'a hapless victim of society's ills'.

The letter received wide support and struck a welcome note of optimism in saying the resort's fortunes could still be turned around. The letter was even praised by Tony Williams, the leader of the council's Tory opposition. 'It could have been written by a Conservative,' he said. Feel free to think up your own damning-with-faint-praise joke.

[ROVING REPORT]

Last time I visited Blackpool, like every other time, it was raining. Mind you, although plenty of people looked miserable, slouching under hoodies and scowling, plenty more admirable old ladies were out defying the wind with meticulously curled and tinted hair protected under plastic shawls, and big smiles on their faces.

One old couple stopped me when they saw me taking a picture of a dead pigeon. They wanted to tell me where I could get a few other grimy shots. 'It's the in thing, isn't it,

delapidation? We get all kinds of arty types with their cameras now. Be sure to have a good time while you're here, mind. Have a bag of chips.'

I took their advice and went to a chippy – and yes, it was delicious. And when I went out to take more photos, yet more people offered me friendly advice – and everyone stayed out of the way politely as I took the shot. I left thinking that the locals are lovely, even if the visitors misbehave.

As I was having those pleasant thoughts, I almost drove into a police roadblock. They were pulling people over and testing them for alcohol. It looked as if they'd caught a few too. Which was pretty unnerving. It was 2pm on a Tuesday.
Sam

㉗ WREXHAM

Motto: Labor omnia vincit (Labour win everything here)
Population: 64,000
Average house price: £202,000
Famous residents: Ricky Tomlinson

The place where grannies spit on the floor.
Dale Jones

CRAP TOWN UPDATE!

PREVIOUS POSITION: 23
REASONS:
• Intimidation of local whistleblowers.
• Production of weak beer.
• Race riots.
RECENT DEVELOPMENTS:
• Wrexham has applied for city status three times since the turn of the millennium. It has been turned down three times.

26 BACUP

**Motto: Honor et industria (Honour and keeping busy)
Population: 13,000
Average house price: £136,000
Famous residents: Beatrice Webb (social reformer), Juliet Bravo (1980s TV Cop)**

Bacup claims to be one of the best preserved mill towns in Northern England, but only in the sense that it's full of empty shells. The shoe and slipper industry died off and the only mill left is the Bacup Sock Company.

Plenty of the town's shops are boarded up too. Much of the 1980s cop show *Juliet Bravo* was filmed here, including the frontage of the real Bacup cop shop which is now – you guessed it – boarded up. Also filmed here were many scenes of that series about daft locals,

The League of Gentlemen. Inspiration was not hard to find.

Bacup also long claimed to have the shortest street on Britain – Elgin Street – but recently lost the title to Ebeneezer Place, an even shorter street in Wick, to the fury of locals, who complained to the local press that the Scottish rival was only 'a corner'.

Tellingly, with a population of 13,000, Bacup has only one independent greengrocer but three tattooists.
Mike North

PUZZLING

An anagram of Bacup is Bollocks. Well, if you came from Bacup, you'd fall for that.
Michael Ashford

CRAP TOWNS TRIVIA

NUTTERS!

The Coconutters are a troupe of dancers who perform in the streets of Bacup every Easter Saturday, in blackface. Their website explains that they have blackened faces in reflection of a pagan or medieval custom that prevented evil spirits recognizing the dancers after they had performed. Or that maybe it reflects local mining connections. Or perhaps because the dance originated with Moorish pirates. It is not, repeat not, because they are racist

town hall

㉕ GREAT YARMOUTH

Motto: Rex et nostra jura (The King and our rights)
Population: 47,000
Average house price: £138,000
Famous residents: Hannah from S Club 7, Jim Davidson

Few towns have been named with such irony as 'Great' Yarmouth.

The trouble with Great Yarmouth isn't the poverty. It isn't the endemic, embedded, unemployment (so bad that the local paper branded the town the 'Shame of Norfolk'). It isn't the drinkers, the druggers or muggers. It isn't even the failing artists, lured there by cheap house prices and never quite having the wherewithal to escape again. No, the real problem is regret. This could and should be one of the most beautiful towns in Europe.

The story that is most often repeated about Yarmouth's decline is that it fell victim to cheap flights and package holidays. Its

chilly promenades couldn't compete with the Costa del Sol, and so they gradually emptied. There's some truth there. But it wasn't planes that knocked down some of Yarmouth's finest buildings and allowed others to sink back into the sea. It wasn't planes that saw some of the finest art-deco architecture in the country and covered it up with gaudy pink and yellow and blue neon frontages. It wasn't planes that stuck a huge slot-machine arcade directly in front of The Hippodrome, Britain's only

CRAP TOWNS TRIVIA In August 2000 a rain of dead sprats fell on Great Yarmouth.

surviving enclosed circus building. It wasn't planes that turned the lovely mini-Moulin Rouge, the Windmill Theatre, into a 12-hole crazy golf course. It wasn't planes. It was morons.

And thanks to these lunatic planning decisions, Great Yarmouth now resembles Elizabeth Taylor in her final days. Years of excess, abusive men and hanging out with deranged pop has-beens has rendered the place mad, sad and dangerous. Every so often you worry that you'll find wee sloshing around her feet. Every so often you get a glimpse of its former beauty, underneath the fright wig, gaudy make-up and crazy pink frock.

'Ken Mod'

㉔ NEWHAVEN

**Population: 12,000
Average house
price: £250,000
Famous residents:
Charles Wells (the
man who broke the
Monte Carlo casino)**

Newhaven. It isn't particularly
new. And it definitely isn't
a haven.

Once a small fishing village, Newhaven was
expanded in the 19th century into a haphazard
collection of streets that look like three minor
suburbs in search of a town.

And now? Well, imagine you are a French
person travelling to England for the first time,
sailing from the picturesque Norman port of
Dieppe to the ferry terminal at Newhaven.
After several hours at sea, your excitement
grows, as the hazy outline of the South Downs
and the white Seven Sisters cliffs becomes
clearer and you become impatient to set foot
on English soil.

DEAD CERTAINTY
When Lord Lucan disappeared in 1974,
his car was discovered in Newhaven; its
presence in the town lending considerable
weight to the theory that he killed himself.

CRAP
TOWNS
TRIVIA

But as soon as the ferry reaches its destination, you see a scene of abandonment and desolation. It looks like a major war has taken place while you were sipping your glass of Bordeaux in the ferry bar: crumbling warehouses with smashed-out windows, vast piles of rusting metal and disused machinery. Bienvenue à Newhaven.

Newhaven's one concession to French visitors is a road sign pointing the way to the 'Centre-Ville', but, unless you count an oversized traffic island that houses a collection of run-down shops, Newhaven has no centre. It is a failed town. The best thing any visitor can do is pass straight through and visit nearby Lewes or Brighton. Or, come to think of it, turn back to France.

Some depressed towns have been revived with a grand building project, like an art gallery or museum – Newhaven got an incinerator.

Steerforth

[ROVING REPORT]

I went to Newhaven on a cold, grey day. I was wrapped up in a thick coat, with hat and gloves and, yes, thermal underwear – and I was still freezing. Most of the other people I saw were wearing shorts and T-shirts. One posed laughingly for a photo and joked about how much he normally charged 'paps' like me. I liked him. One threatened to set me on fire for taking photos. I was less sure about him. One was standing outside a pub near the water's edge, holding a can, shouting 'Bitch! Bitch! Bitch!' into the biting wind. Him, I avoided. Seagulls cried. Somewhere in the distance a bell clanged. Across the dirty water, there was a huge rubbish tip. I left.

Sam

㉓ DURSLEY

Motto: God with us
Population: 6,000
Average house
price: £225,000
Famous residents:
William Tyndale
(martyr, burned at the stake in 1536)

The name says it all. The town is as wrong as it sounds. Once a pretty rural village, Dursley has been left to decay until it has all the appeal of an Elizabethan's teeth.

The old market place has become dominated by concrete and vacant charity shops. The new Sainsbury's supermarket has left a ten-foot wall and an acre of paving that recalls the best of 1950s planning design, where the drabness of the locals' tweed jackets is echoed in the fusty beige of the concrete slabs.

Substance abuse generally involves mainlining crazy amounts of sugar during the day. And at twilight the plastic gangstas venture out. 'Yo, blood!' and 'Sick!' they shout, in a Cotswold accent with overtones of Croydon-Cockney, proving that the youth culture is as confused as the planning.

Laz

CRAP TOWNS TRIVIA

WIZARD

JK Rowling, who was born in nearby Yate, named a family in her mega-selling Harry Potter saga after this town. It wasn't a compliment. The Dursley family are unpleasant snobs who force Harry to sleep in a cupboard under the stairs.

22 MEDWAY TOWNS

Population: 257,000
Average house price: £165,000
Famous residents: Charles Dickens, Billy Childish, Kelly Brook

Observant readers will have noticed the 's' in the title of this entry. Strictly speaking the Medway isn't one town, it's a collection of them. But they are all awful, and lots of people don't like them, so here they are.

VERSION 1

Medway. My home conurbation that squats on the greasy bank of the eponymous river. The site of the first youth prison, Borstal (so called because it was built in Borstal village in Rochester), Gillingham Football Club, the Dockyard (where they built HMS *Victory*), Medway College of Art (Tracey Emin studied here) and the Strand, a marvellous leisure park consisting of rusting swings, an outdoor swimming pool and a miniature train. Lovely.

Medway plies its historical re-enactments and ancient buildings with all the vim and vigour of a member of the WI on Adderall posing nude for charidee; but should you make the mistake of venturing out after dark, it shrugs off this genteel middle-England mask and reveals a lethal truth. The Medway towns turn out a rough lot, all tooled up and ready for the off. You'd be surprised what one can conceal in a knock-off Louis Vuitton clutch bag – and don't even think about the menfolk.

You've been warned. If you do find yourself here and want to go shopping, you're fucked. Rochester High Street is packed full of teashops, pedlars of antiques and hairdressers. Chatham High Street and the Pentagon Centre are full of pound shops and mothers cursing at their little children. Allders is in receivership. Marks and Spencer and all those other high street favourites have

Medway Towns photo: Joe Dunbar

moved out to Bluewater, the shopping and leisure centre of your dreams. And it's here that you will find the more mobile residents of Medway, blissfully consuming in the perpetual sunshine of the sterile mall with a tight little smile on their faces.

VERSION 2

The Medway Towns are rotten. Everyone has fucked off to Bluewater.

Heidi James-Dunbar

MEDWAY DEFENDED! KILMARNOCK ATTACKED!

I moved to Medway from a really truly crap town in Scotland on the west coast where heroin addicts and stabbings as well as naff football violence and pound shops are also aplenty. You really should go visit Kilmarnock, you'll run back to Medway on the first decrepit Russian sub you can hitch a ride on.

The New Maid of Kent

㉑ KILMARNOCK

Motto: Make it Kilmarnock
Population: 45,000
Average house price: £147,000
Famous residents: Ben and James Johnston, drummer and bassist of Scottish rock band Biffy Clyro, Johnnie Walker whisky

In 2004 the *Rough Guide to Scotland* described Kilmarnock as 'shabby and depressed'. The guide noted it was 'saddled with some terrible shopping centres'. It also remarked on 'a grim one-way system'. It's got worse since then.

A town leading the charge for our latest foray into recession. Once an industrial powerhouse, famed internationally for its carpets (production ceased in the town in 2005), Kilmarnock is now a post-industrial wasteland, with much of its once-handsome

Kilmarnock is home to a building called the Dick Institute. Sadly, it isn't what you're thinking. It's a museum and library.

town centre bulldozed since the Second World War. Nowadays the main shopping drag is a grim, litter-strewn wind tunnel, with nary an outlet that isn't a pound shop or a pawnbroker. An apology for sophisticated cafe culture is provided, meanwhile, by a lone and shabby-looking branch of Costa Coffee. Even these delights, however, are hard to access; the town itself is ringed by a growth of dirty-grey pebble-dashed flats of unspeakable misery – the sort that all Scottish towns appear to have at their edges, presumably to repel visitors.

On the day I last visited, the Olympic torch was passing through the town; the whole event felt like a vast and ill-judged pity party. Worse yet, the festivities meant that surrounding roads were closed off, making escape nigh on impossible. The time we spent threading our way through sorry-looking light-industrial estates and shut-down high

streets will never be got back.
Sarah

KILMARNOCK DEFENDED!
Aye you're mebbe right, but I bet you can't big a can o Tennent's in one go like folk here can. And as for Buckfast . . .
Analise

CRAP TOWNS TRIVIA

COMMOTION LOTION
One bottle of Buckfast Tonic Wine contains as much caffeine as eight cans of Coke and has a 15 per cent ABV. The drink, also known as Buckie, also known as Wreck the Hoose Juice, also known as Commotion Lotion, also known as Trampagne, also known as Loopy Juice, was linked to 5,638 crimes in the Strathclyde police area between 2006 and 2009. One in 10 of those offences had been violent and 114 of them involved the use of a Buckfast bottle as a weapon. Buckfast is made by Benedictine monks in Devon. When a Scottish health minister complained that the drink was causing problems, its distributors accused him of 'bad manners' and 'a complete lack of judgement'.

⓴ WOODSTOCK

Motto: Dieu defend le droit (God defends right-wingers)
Population: 2,900
Average house price: £453,000
Famous residents: Winston Churchill (deceased)

No, not that one. The other one. The little place near Oxford. The one with Blenheim Palace and all the gift shops . . .

Woodstock is a town for people who have looked at nearby Oxford and thought: 'What this place really needs is more shops selling teddies, heritage crockery and Union Jack bunting. And fewer interesting people.'

Here, a two-bedroom house will cost you over £300,000, and finding a parking space at the weekend will cost you your sanity. But it isn't the tourist tat or the crazy prices that hurt the most. The cruellest thing about Woodstock is its name: a constant reminder of how much better things could be. In America they have Bob Dylan, The Band, brown acid and a legendary free festival. Here we have long-dead aristocrats, the WI, tea shops and local Tory Party fundraisers.

David Young

[BAD COUNCIL]

Early in 2012 simmering tensions in Woodstock Parish Council broke out into outright war. There was a fierce argument over the decision to obtain a wedding licence for a second room in the town hall, furious dissent over an increase in rents to a local bowls and tennis club, and, according to council member Victoria Edwards, councillors even embarked on an endless round of bickering over the question of whether to install a loft ladder in the council HQ. Eventually Edwards resigned, telling the papers: 'Woodstock is like the Mad Hatter's Tea Party. There are lots of cliques and petty vested interests . . . It is *The Vicar of Dibley* with nasty bits thrown in . . . The council is not fit for purpose. All it is fit for is putting up the Christmas lights.'

Emma Jay joined

Edwards in handing in her resignation. Jay said, 'It is well known that parish councils tend to be filled with people with not enough else to to do, who are rather pleased with the sound of their own voice, and sure of the rightness of their point of view. Woodstock is no different. But Woodstock is blessed in addition with a few councillors with some more dangerous traits: an extraordinary degree of control freakery, an enthusiasm for conspiracy theories, caucus meetings and gang voting and a relish for stirring rows and schism . . . because of the baleful influence of a few councillors, the place is toxic. I cannot bear any more of it. With my blood pressure to consider, I don't need the grief. I quit.'

⑲ CRAWLEY

Motto: I grow and I rejoice
Population: 100,000
Average house price: £198,000
Famous residents: The Cure

Crawley's motto, I grow and I rejoice, might be good for a willy – but no one is actually pleased about the new town's outward creep.

Once a small, sleepy place on the way to Brighton, Crawley became identified as a potential new town after the end of the Second World War and by the late 1950s the population had increased fivefold, largely due

to an influx of people from the East End of London. At first, it was even regarded as one of the more successful new towns, providing thousands of jobs and affordable homes. But that was because it hadn't yet been completely ruined by Brutalist architecture and high-rise developments. It was more like a dull, Outer London suburb that had been dropped onto some fields in Sussex.

Soon Crawley became the victim of its own success and, in the 1960s, permission was given to double the town's population to over 100,000. Today, Crawley is characterised by cheap, poorly designed housing, a creaking transport infrastructure and a cultural life that makes Milton Keynes look like the Weimar Republic.

Now, the town is populated by people who think Karl Popper is a designer label and that Mansfield Park is where Nottingham Forest play.

Steerforth

NEW AGE BOLLOCKS

I once went to a Psychic Fair in Crawley. A woman dangled a crystal over my crotch and told me she could 'feel a lump there'. That was a decade ago and I still don't have cancer so I'm guessing the lump she felt was just one of my balls.

Tom Cox

18 HAWORTH

Population: 6,000
Average house
price: £185,000
Famous residents:
Charlotte, Emily
and Anne Brontë
(all deceased)

The Brontë sisters, it's fair to say, were miserable. Their brother Branwell was suicidally self-destructive. Why? They lived in Haworth.

With mislaid sentimentality we thank Haworth for giving us the Brontë sisters. Really we should be cursing the place for killing them so young. It was Haworth's unsanitary conditions and hard living that did for them. During the famous sisters' brief lives, the town was an open sewer; the main street a river of poo, wee – and worse. There were so many deaths in the

town that the graveyard filled beyond capacity. Seepage from the corpses poisoned the local water supply – creating more bodies.

It's a miracle that the Brontë sisters lived as long as they did. At least they all made it into their thirties. The average life expectancy among their neighbours was a nasty, brutish and short 25.8 years. But if they'd lived elsewhere they might have had full and happy lives. And we'd probably have been saved a great many mawkish costume dramas.

And I know it sounds unfair to criticise the town for something it did to folk who died almost two centuries ago. But then, in Haworth they're still doing everything they can to make it feel like it's still the 1850s. Short of poisoning the water . . .

'Branwell'

CRAP TOWNS TRIVIA

DAYLIGHT ROBBERY

In 2003 Carstoppers, a clamping firm controlling car parks in Haworth, was given the Dick Turpin award by the RAC. According to the RAC executive director Edmund King: 'They were singled out for their dogged determination and lack of goodwill.' The company clamped a car while the driver was asleep inside and fined a wheelchair user for arriving late at a car park at the top of a hill.

At the time, Ted Evans, the owner of Carstoppers, said he 'absolutely' refuted that any vehicles were wrongly clamped. Since then, his firm has also hit the headlines for clamping former House of Commons Speaker Betty Boothroyd, clamping a minibus taking special needs children on an outing, and because a company employee was threatened with an ASBO thanks to his enthusiastic ticketing activities.

[BAD COUNCIL]

TO GET TO TOP WITHINS FARM, THE SUPPOSED INSPIRATION FOR WUTHERING HEIGHTS, YOU HAVE TO WALK UP PENISTONE HILL AND ON TOWARDS DICK DELF HILL. STOP SNIGGERING.

WITHERING SLEIGHTS

The countryside surrounding Haworth is beautiful and much of the town itself has a rugged old-fashioned charm. But don't worry, the local council have got plans!

The village is already swamped by ugly new housing developments and recently, a local development framework document released by Bradford Council identified 14 potential development sites around Haworth.

John Huxley, the chairman of the parish council, said: 'The document says it wants to preserve and promote Haworth as a tourist destination. After all, it's perhaps second in England only to Stratford. Then, just a few pages on, it says we have to have new housing estates. There is an assault on the Brontë landscape going on.'

⑰ BRIGHTON

Motto: Inter undas et colles floremus (Let us be like flowers between the waves and the hills)
Population: 166,000
Average house price: £302,500
Famous residents: Fatboy Slim, Pinkie from *Brighton Rock*, Julie Burchill

It's pretty. It's fun. It's cosmopolitan. It's tolerant. It's handy for London. It's by the sea. And yet . . .

There is nothing about Brighton as a location I dislike particularly – it's very pretty, there are various interesting things to look at, nice quirky little shops, and always something going on if you can afford it and so on. It is just that a huge number of the people who live there are massive cocks.

Of course, cocks scatter the planet profusely, but whereas in the average town I would say the ratio of cocks to non-cocks is about 1:3, in Brighton that ratio is, at the very least, reversed. If you are a Brighton resident and reading this, it is statistically likely that you are a massive cock. If you are not, then it is almost inevitable that a good number of your friends are. You may want to look into this.

It is very hard to leave your home and go out and do something in Brighton without someone, somewhere ruining things by behaving in a cock-like manner. Notable events that stick out in my memory include the time the shop assistant in a bakery kept me waiting for several minutes as he shouted 'Are you the mayor?' repeatedly at a passing man who quite obviously was the mayor. Or the day I went to the library to do some research only to find I couldn't, as someone had booked the pedestrian area outside for a drum ensemble to play and advertise chocolate. Or more recently, when I made a regrettable return visit with my baby daughter, only to find that in Brighton a pavement is considered an excellent location for a brawl, regardless of whether someone is pushing a baby in a buggy down it at the time.

Even in my Brighton home, I was not free of cocks. The landlord of the flat below me had a strict 'cocks-only' policy when renting it out. The first resident was the owner of a pair of enormous Dalmatians, who ran around his tiny flat crashing into things all day while he shouted 'No more food!' every minute or so. If, however, I so much as accidentally dropped a magazine on the floor, he would shout up, convinced that every slight noise was an act of aggression against him. The next resident was a *Dad's Army* obsessive, and would leave the menu screen of his DVD on for hours at a time, the volume loud, and the theme tune repeating over and over. Sometimes he wasn't even in.

One incident in particular sums up my time in Brighton. The neighbours next door decided to have an all-night party, completely unannounced, in which they pumped music at top volume into their garden where they had lit a sizeable bonfire. When it became clear they were not going to allow anybody any sleep that night, I went round to request that they wrap it up. I was given this reply: 'You've got to expect this type of thing. It's Brighton.'

This is the logic of utterly selfish hedonism, devoid of consideration or even awareness of others, that permeates so much of Brighton. It is a playground for children who have never grown up. But not just any children. You remember the ones I mean from when you were growing up. Those children who were cocks.

Spencer Macleavy

SLAUGHTERED

The historical nickname for Brighton – 'Queen of Slaughtering Places' – may be a considered an overly regal one, conjuring up glory days of yonder that included the infamous trunk murders and death-by-chocolates murderess Christiana Edwards. Now what's left is a city that can boast having the highest drug-related death count and second highest suicide rate in England. It also has several areas that can proudly boast as being in the top 1 per cent for deprivation in the country. Anyone in the south who wonders how grim it really is up north need only make the short journey to Brighton.

I am fortunate to live in one of the more salubrious areas, and yet am not allowed to go to sleep until 3am some weeknights due to the ketamine-dealing, music-pumping couple and their crying child who live on one side. I then get woken up at 7.30am on the dot by the sounds of the wife-beater on the other side verbally and/or physically abusing his partner. We looked out into the shoddy back garden in the morning the other day and saw the next-door toddler walking around with a fag in its mouth.

Anon (please!)

CRAP TOWN UPDATE!

PREVIOUS POSITION: 22
REASONS:
• Bad trip hop, bad face hair, shocking inequality, trying and failing to be Barcelona.
RECENT DEVELOPMENTS:
• Trip hop has disappeared. Bad facial hair grows ever more prevalent thanks to an influx of hipsters.
• In the first edition of *Crap Towns* there was a report on the failure of anyone to rebuild the town's once-beautiful West Pier and surprising local opposition to its repair (particularly from the owners of the other pier in town). Back in 2003, the pier had received £1.7 million in lottery funds, planning permission had finally been granted to carry out the necessary work

– and a mysterious fire had suddenly broken out and made that work impossible.

More recently, a millionaire property developer offered £25 million to rebuild the pier – but withdrew the offer when the West Pier Trust, the organization supposedly looking after the structure, cast doubts on his plans. Curiously, Glynn Jones, chair of the trust, said it was essential any scheme to rebuild the pier did not clash with the building of a gigantic observation tower nearby, the i360. Locals were then surprised to note that the section of the West Pier Trust's own website dedicated to 'the future' featured many plans for the i360 and artists' impressions of how it will look – none of which feature a restored pier.

⓰ BANBURY

Motto: Dominus nobis sol et scutum (Our lord is the sun and a shield)
Population: 45,000
Average house price: £195,000
Famous residents: Gordon Ramsay, John Craven, Anthony Burgess, Paul Gadd

A town famous for being mentioned in an old song, having a cross and pretty much nothing else.

LOAD OF COCK

Some time in the 12th century a person unknown rode to Banbury Cross on a cock horse. According to the nursery rhyme, this person went to see a 'fine lady' (also unknown) who sat upon a white horse, who had rings on her fingers and bells on her toes, and who was accompanied by 'fine music'

wherever she went. Variations on the story also had the first person buying some bread for a penny and an apple pie for two pennies.

Ever since, most people have wondered why such a big thing should be made of such apparently insignificant events. But then, most people haven't experienced life in Banbury. I have – 15 long years of it – and believe me, if a stranger had relieved the tedium by riding into town with bells on her toes, I'd also be trying to commemorate it in song.

'Lady Godiva'

EVEN SHITTER

'Ride a Cock Horse to Banbury Cross' isn't the town's only musical connection. Paul Francis Gadd was also born here in 1944. He went on to become Gary Glitter – internationally famous glam rock star and convicted paedophile.

John West

CRAP TOWNS TRIVIA

CROSSED OFF

The most interesting thing in Banbury is the stone cross – which isn't very interesting at all. It isn't even very old. It was built in 1859. The cross celebrated in the famous song disappeared centuries earlier.

YES, A LETTER HAS DROPPED OFF

⓯ PONTEFRACT

**Motto: Post mortem patris pro filio
(After Dad's dead, go for the son)
Population: 29,000
Average house price £160,000
Famous residents: Richard II (who
was murdered in town), Harold
Shipman (who murdered in town)**

Thanks to its sandy soil the West Yorkshire market town of Pontefract was one of the few places in Britain able to grow licorice. Thanks to globalization, it doesn't grow any now. And everything else seems to have died too.

*Pomfret, Pomfret! O thou bloody prison,
Fatal and ominous to noble peers!
Within the guilty closure of thy walls
Richard the second here was hack'd to death;
And, for more slander to thy dismal seat,
We give thee up our guiltless blood to drink.*

The words are Shakespeare's. The poet conjures a gruesome vision of a grim Northern fastness; a place of suffering, humiliation and death. That was 1591. It hasn't improved since.

It says something profound about the character of a town when its worldwide renown rests upon an ancient remedy for constipation. And although Sir John Betjeman might once have waxed lyrical about 'The Liquorice Fields of Pontefract', the fields in question have long since been deposited onto the dung heap of history along with Pontefract Cakes, Liquorice Allsorts and other assorted purgatives now made wholly from imported stuff. Betjeman also described 'tanneries, mills and shuttered corner shops', but now only the shutters remain. Here, regeneration is something that happens to other people.

Still, there is a ruined castle (knocked down by Oliver Cromwell who, regrettably, stopped at that), alongside a couple of churches and a pedestrianised precinct dominated by an 18th-century Buttercross. This attractive structure was once a market shelter for farmers' wives and their baskets of dairy

Pontefract was given its name by the Romans. It means 'broken bridge'. That's right. Even 2,000 years ago, stuff there didn't work properly.

produce. It is now a place to spit and swear while feasting on sausage rolls and pasties.

With the historic cattle market formerly known as Kiko's discotheque now an empty shell haunted only by the shadows of the past (most of them drinking stale beer and going without knickers), options for an evening's entertainment are limited to what is generally reckoned to be the country's highest concentration of public houses per square mile. Here one can sup local ales with muscular young men in unfeasibly tight T-shirts and engage in earnest philosophical banter – usually some variant of the following moral paradox: 'Are you looking at our lass? No? Why, what's up wi' her?'

Mind you, cultural sophisticates who lack the stomach for drink-fuelled violence need not entirely despair. For even in Pontefract the throbbing pulse of multi-cultural metropolitan glamour is never all that far removed. Yes, Wakefield 's only half an hour up the road . . .

'Richard III'

⑭ THETFORD

**Motto: Antiq burg de Thetford (Thetford is old)
Population: 22,000
Average house price: £158,000
Famous residents: Thomas Paine, Maharajah Duleep Singh**

For a sleepy Norfolk town, Thetford has had a huge impact on human history. But only because Thomas Paine, its most famous son, hated the place so passionately.

Thetford was the birthplace of Thomas Paine, aka the Father of the American Revolution. He was the author of *Common Sense* and *The Rights of Man*. He was a tireless campaigner. He was one of history's greatest political thinkers and an eloquent proponent of social justice, emancipation and liberty. Without Thetford and Thomas Paine there would have been no D-Day Landings, no walking on the moon, no Elvis Presley. And no Sarah Palin, Fox News, Intercontinental Ballistic Missiles, Guantanamo Bay, 60-inch-waist 'pants', or people who can't say lieutenant properly, either.

Tom was, in short, a big deal. The kind of man you'd think might deserve a statue. Unless, of course, you happen to be one of Thetford's many local Tories. When a group of Americans first offered to erect a statue to the great man in the 1960s, a Conservative town councillor declared it 'an insult to the town' and tried to stop its erection. When that failed, his council tried to get an inscription about Paine being a 'traitor' engraved alongside the current inscription: 'My country is the world, my religion is to do good.' Ever since, the town has regarded its famous son as a source of shame, rather than pride.

But don't worry! The dislike was mutual. Thetford was a thoroughly Rotten Borough in Paine's day. It was dominated by a small, rich elite, who frequently (and literally) got away with murder, while poor men could be hanged for stealing a sheep. He hated it.

In fact, you could probably say that the entire American Revolution was a result of Paine's desire to escape the legacy of his upbringing in Thetford. And you can definitely say that one of his most famous quotes is about the town: 'When, in countries that are called civilised, we see age going to the workhouse and youth to the gallows, something must be wrong in the system of government.'

John Bunn

A CORRECTION

I don't think it's fair to criticise Thetford because Thomas Paine didn't like it 200 years ago. Not least because it makes the place seem far more interesting than it actually is. He's the last notable person that the town has produced.

Life here was getting so dull by the 1950s

that the council actually applied to London County Council to bring businesses to the town – and people. Like a shot, LCC offloaded thousands of its most problematic families onto the hitherto sleepy Norfolk town, adding addiction and unrest to the traditional local problem of inbreeding. Soon afterwards the local council also decided that the centre of town wasn't ugly enough and built a new mainstreet of flat-roofed, flat-fronted, squat and brutal retail sheds.

Following local government reorganization in the 1970s, the town council lost the power to make most decisions – but by then the damage had been done. We've been enjoying that legacy ever since.
'Lafayette'

CORRECTION CORRECTED
Actually, there have been plenty of notable people in Thetford since Thomas Paine's day – even if they were largely held here against their will.

Most of *Dad's Army* was filmed on the quiet local streets and there was an even more impressive local in the form of Maharajah Duleep Singh, the last royal ruler of the Punjab. He was exiled to nearby Elveden in the 19th century and there's a very fine new statue of him in town.

True, he didn't like it much there. Naturally enough he spent most of his days pining for his homeland, desperate to flee Thetford. (Which he did, eventually, making it as far as Paris, where he died.)

Mind you, it is at least fun to imagine what Paine might think of Thetford's latest piece of statuary. The birthplace of one of history's most persuasive republicans has become a place of pilgrimage for devotees of the Sikh royal. And that isn't the cruellest irony. Tom Paine might at last have a statue in Thetford, but it has been so positioned that he gazes out

forever over the town's main thoroughfare: King Street.
Sam

PHALLIC ATTACK
My friends and I once spent an evening in Thetford. Some people threw a cucumber at us.
Zoe H

⓭ CAMBERLEY

Motto: A deo et regina (From God and the Queen) **Population:** 31,000 **Average house price:** £398,000

Famous residents: Bros (famously bad teen-pop band), Five Star (famously bad teen-pop band), 5ive (famously even worse teen-pop band), Piggy from *Lord of the Flies*

....

Despite its rich musical legacy and wealthy inhabitants, Camberley is a town people aspire to leave.

At an earlier early stage of its development, Daniel Defoe pooh-poohed the area as, 'horrid and frightful to look on; not only good for little but good for nothing'. But things have changed since then. They've built a mall.

And Camberley has an

illustrious and rich musical culture with past residents including such trend-setters as Five Star, 5ive, Richard Stilgoe and the creepy Midwich-twins from Bros all the way down to Rick Wakeman.

If the thought of a Five Star–5ive–Richard Stilgoe super-group hasn't already got your toes tapping, how about humming along to the tender melody of the Broadmoor siren which is unleashed at 10am every Monday? Commencing in the Sixties and originally intended to alert the town's residents to the escape of an inmate (or vice versa), it now serves primarily as a means of waking up local school children half way through double physics.

Another notable Camberley alumnus is the not coincidentally named Camberley Kate, who

spent most of the Seventies prowling round the town centre scaring children with a pack of thirty or so formerly stray dogs tied to a green cart with bits of string. The locals, who tend to distrust 'characters' and dislike dog crap, often complained, but the police were apparently grateful that she kept so many dogs off the streets. She tied them up outside Sainsbury's instead. Kate told the press she 'preferred dogs to humans', and who in Camberley could blame her?

In the 19th century Camberley gained a reputation for clean air on account of the many pines in the locality. Victorian environmental friendliness indeed – but fear not, the trees have now largely been chopped down. A report published in 2009 revealed that Camberley had the biggest CO_2 footprint of any town in the UK with an impressive 28.05 tonnes per household. And if that's not

something to shout about, I don't know what is. Take that, South Shields!

To date, no monument to this staggering achievement has been unveiled but perhaps the most notable landmark that Camberley has to offer is the irony-free white elephant, constructed wholly from drain and sewerage pipes, which can be glimpsed from the A30 as you drive swiftly out of town heading south-west towards the bright lights of Basingstoke.

Or there's the mall.
Andy Lovett

GONE POSTAL

Whilst other towns have derived their names from attractive local features (Watford from the ford over the river Wat; Sevenoaks from, well, seven oaks), Camberley, in an early example of corporate branding, was originally named Cambridge Town when a local speculator built the Cambridge Hotel there. The name was only changed to assist geographically-challenged 19th-century posties who struggled to distinguish the Surrey-based interloper from its more illustrious namesake a mere 86 miles away. The arse and the elbow are differently named for the same reason.
Andy Lovett

CRAP TOWNS TRIVIA

⑫ JAYWICK

**Population: 5,000
Average house
price: £138,000
Famous residents:
None. Although
General Custard
comes from nearby Clacton**

Contrary to popular prejudice Essex isn't all about bling, blondes, and drunk fat-faced bankers puking at Liverpool Street Station before catching the late train to Billericay. It's also about grinding poverty and shaming inequality.

Our holiday, from the initial internet research, sounded too good to be true: a caravan site located right next to the sea, with miles of sandy beaches. A site just one mile from the 'pretty village of St Osyth' – which, statistically, is the driest, sunniest place in the whole of the UK. And

rock-bottom prices as well? Something's up, surely?

Yep.

One day, I decided to walk the three miles along the 'promenade' to Clacton. There you find miles and miles of beach – but not really the sandy kind, more the sand-and-pebbles-and-sea-holly-and-dogshit-and-syringes kind. Within minutes of starting, I was passing the coastal front of the town of Jaywick. Nothing had prepared me for the experience.

For every house with a proud elderly couple, be-deckchaired, sipping tea and surrounded by gnomes, there is another dwelling that is either boarded up, fallen down or burnt out.

Why are there pensioners holidaying in a shanty town, I wondered? Whatever the reason, I quickened my pace, and glanced

nervously down all the 'roads' perpendicular to the beach; most houses had old sofas and televisions piling up in the yard, with broken-down cars blocking the entrances.

The roads themselves are not made of tarmac, they are made of decaying, lopsided slabs of concrete. The houses all look poorly built, patched up over the years with odd, crumbling verandas and bizarre patios on stilts.

But the most striking thing of all about Jaywick was the lack of people – this was midday, and it was virtually a ghost town. If it wasn't for the odd hunched-backed old woman scurrying nervously past me, I could well have been in downtown Chernobyl.

I looked the place up when I got back from holiday, and here are the facts: Jaywick was created by a dodgy London wide-boy before the war who bought up a barren area of land, threw up tiny houses as cheaply as possible and marketed them as cheap getaway holiday chalets for the workers. The state of the buildings now is testimony to just how cheaply they must have been constructed. Some of the original Eastenders who bought up their dream affordable home, away from the smoke of London, made it their permanent residence, and now proudly refuse to move in spite of everything else happening around them. And what's happening is that Jaywick has become the place that the London councils and social services relocate problem families and drug addicts to, in the hope they might have some chance of rehabilitation away from the Smoke.

CRAP TOWNS TRIVIA Jaywick was named Britain's most deprived town in 2010. Most of the towns around it are extremely wealthy. Isn't capitalism great?

On the plus side, it's also just about the cheapest place to buy a 'house' in the whole of the UK, which probably explains why the poor bastards who decided to plough their meagre life savings into retiring there cannot afford to leave. It has to be seen to be believed.

Nick Pounder

DETERGENT

Jaywick sounds like something you put down the loo.

Phil

⑪ CALAIS

Population: 74,000
Average house price: €220,000 (£188,000)
Famous residents: Beau Brummel (while in exile from England)

Calais isn't British any more – legally. In spirit, however, it's nearly all ours . . . and nearly all awful.

Yes, I know Calais isn't strictly in the UK – but that's about the best thing you can say for it. In fact, all my French friends say we can have it. We've made it English enough. The town's great misfortune has been its ease of access from Dover. I'm not talking about all those long centuries of marauding armies eager to escape our rain-lashed island, or even the pounding it took in the Second World War.

Calais was actually doing okay until we Brits realised that it was almost as easy for us to reach as our local supermarkets – and able to supply us with plonk and beer at far cheaper prices.

Back when sterling was strong against the euro, booze cruisers from Britain wrecked this town. We filled it with gigantic cold warehouses, with red-faced men lugging around beer kegs almost as absurdly huge as their bellies and with endless chattering, clattering, giggling women topping up on fizz and puking on the pavements. We even once sent Chris Evans. Unfortunately he didn't stay long, but he did live broadcast his own alcohol shopping and so encourage even more people to visit.

But the worst of it wasn't all the bargain hunters and alcoholics. It wasn't even all the outsize Tescos and shops named after soap operas that looked like ruined fairground rides and where even the staff refused to speak French. No. It was the fact that we all stopped coming. As soon as the pound collapsed, we shoved off, leaving economic ruin, rotting warehouses, and endless empty car parks. It now looks almost as bad as Swindon.

Francis De Guise

CRAP TOWNS TRIVIA

LEADEN VERSE Calais became an English possession in 1347 when Edward III took over the town after an 11-month siege. We were good at annoying the French back then too. We evacuated the town of all locals and taunted them by hanging the following rhyme over the gates:

'Then shalle the frenchmen Calais winne When iron and leade lyke corke shall swimme.'

This was proved wrong in 1558 when Francis, Duke of Guise, stormed the garrison and recaptured the city. Queen Mary was bitterly disappointed by the loss and said: 'When I am dead and opened, you shall find "Calais" lying in my heart.' That didn't happen either.

10

STOKE-ON-TRENT

Motto: Vis unita fortior (Strength united is more strong)
Population: 240,000
Average house price: £165,000
Famous residents: Neil Morrissey, Frank Bough, Anthea Turner, Bruno Brookes

Once a byword for industry, ingenuity and fancy stuff made out of clay, Stoke-on-Trent has more recently become a prime example of industrial decline and stagnation.

Stoke has become a city in which disappointment in the past has mutated into a sneering resentment of the present. It was in Stoke in the 1990s that I heard a shopkeeper complaining about decimal currency.

It was once a thriving industrial city; it was never wealthy, but it was wealthy enough,

89

and it had an industrial pride, confidence, and swagger. But the decline of the pottery industry, the destruction of the coal industry, and the closure of the Shelton Bar Steel Works tore the heart from the place.

There is one growth industry: warehousing. The economic hopes of the region have been pinned on the provision of large, empty buildings into which things can be put. As you head into the city by train from the north, you can see a large green warehouse on the left. It is in the middle of nowhere, and was completed a couple of years ago. It is still empty.

I have several doctor friends who have commented that working at the North Staffs hospital is fascinating because they see illnesses there that have been eradicated elsewhere for two generations: diseases of pollution and poverty. The hospital itself is built on a plague pit; I had an aunt who would refuse to be admitted there because she could remember it from her childhood, when it had been a workhouse.

Stoke-on-Trent is a city built on coal and clay with a spirit of asbestos.

Enzyme

A GOOD SIGN

I went to Alton Towers with my girlfriend and her mates, and stayed in a hotel in Stoke. When we arrived the first thing the concierge told us was that we shouldn't go out after 7pm if we didn't want to be 'stabbed or sumfink'.

The entire town is coated with a thick dark film of soot and grime, and people seem to actually go out of their way to be nasty or unhelpful. It has only two redeeming features:
1. It isn't Dundee.
2. It has quite possibly the best car wash sign ever, which proudly claims to give 'the best handjobs in town'.

DonMorte

DON'T MENTION THE WAR
A persistent and convincing urban myth has it that no German bombs dropped on Stoke-on-Trent during the Second World War. The reason? After studying aerial photographs, the Luftwaffe decided it had already been bombed.

CRAP TOWNS TRIVIA

blue plaque committee

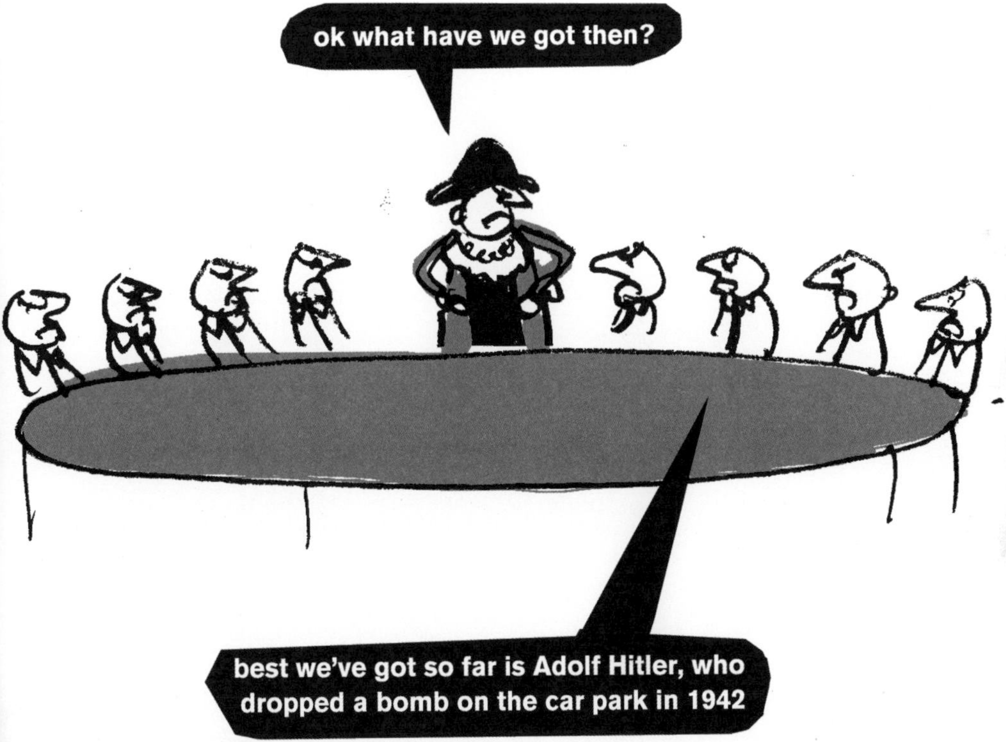

HIGH WYCOMBE

Motto: Industria ditat (Getting busy makes you rich)
Population: 118,000
Average house price: £309,000
Famous residents: Fern Britton, Mel B, Howard Jones, Frankie Vaughn

A commuter town with a derelict town centre, failed local industry, racial tension and absurd house prices. High Wycombe is a big, boring metaphor for the rest of the UK.

High Wycombe isn't entirely bland. It has a chair museum – it used to fart out chairs like it now does hopelessness. The train station also has the largest retaining wall in all of Great Britain, making it ideal for suicides. In spite of these attractions, I left three years ago, and I am never, ever fucking returning.

It wasn't the nightlife that drove me away, although it is utterly abysmal. Wycombe no longer even has a nightclub. The too-bright lights of Pure (formerly Time, formerly Eden, formerly *insert suitably trendy utopic name here*) are no more, long closed by the threats of administration and violence. This club, which coincidentally changed its name every time someone was brutally wounded on the dance floor, and could even list an axe attack in its incident logbook, finally closed its doors in late 2012.

It also wasn't the recession-ravaged skeletal remains of a high street either, or the pound shops and congealed fried chicken outlets (of which

High Wycombe photos: Anwar Patel

High Wycombe has the highest percentage of empty shops in the UK. Meanwhile, its satellites Beaconsfield, Gerrard's Cross and Amersham were named one, two and three in a list of Britain's richest towns in the *Daily Telegraph* in 2008.

a startling number rank at 0 out of 5 on the food hygiene scale). Nor was it the weird smell that exists almost everywhere in High Wycombe; a combination of fast food and pollution from the endless traffic that struggles to escape over the summits of the Chiltern Hills.

Oh no.

Instead it was the unhappy coexistence between the town's two predominant racial groups – poorer South Asian in the central pockets of town, and wealthy *Daily*

Mail-reading white in the suburbs – that made this town such an unhappy place to be. The complete ghettoization of Wycombe that splits the urban area upon almost purely racial lines (when was the last time you saw an Asian face in Tylers Green, and how many white people linger on the streets of Castlefield?) has resulted in ever-brewing racial tension that gets worse year on year. The isolated incidents of racism, which sadly occur more often than the *Bucks Free Press* and Thames Valley Police happily report, and inaccurate prejudice that is traded among both communities behind closed doors has resulted in these ethnic groups really hating each other. Recent news events have featured organised local gangs exploiting young girls for sex; the conviction of Wycombe-based international terrorists and extremists, gang-related knee-cappings and stabbings. The bigoted tripe that spews from the mouths of just about everyone creates an atmosphere of permanent hostility that just makes you want to get out. And once you do, you won't come back.

Curtley West

COMMUTER SAYS NO

If kicking the crap out of other people isn't your thing (I'm assuming that being gang-mugged doesn't appeal to most people either), then living in High Wycombe can only lead in one direction: manic, bi-polar, unparalleled depression.

Maybe it's the lingering influence of the town's formerly booming furniture trade, and the cloud that still hovers over the town's old men who know that their lives can be summed up in the sentence, 'Well, I made some chairs.'

Or could it possibly be the effect of being a commuter town of the highest order? That 70 per cent of its residents couldn't give half a shit about the state of the town or the local social scene. No, they're all busy lining their pockets in London all day and drinking Chateau Yquem in their high-hedged gardens all evening, feeling smug that they don't have to go into the centre of town at all – their maid will do it for them.

Chris Smith

NUNEATON

Motto: United to achieve
Population: 73,000
Average house price: £154,000
Famous residents: Larry Grayson, Jive Bunny, Mary Ann Evans (aka George Eliot)

Nuneaton is a commuter town feeding into Coventry and Birmingham. And is just as exciting as that sounds.

A BIT THICK

For a small town Nuneaton has punched above its weight, culturally speaking. George Eliot was born there and used the environs as the canvas for most of her novels. The Milby of *Scenes of Clerical Life* is a thinly disguised Nuneaton, while the election day riot from *Felix Holt* actually happened in Nuneaton with

a teenage Mary Ann Evans as a witness. The life of the town is thus woven into the work of one of the English language's greatest novelists.

And how does the town commemorate this? By promoting her literature? No, it does it by naming every fixed structure after her.

There's a George Eliot school, a George Eliot pub, a George Eliot hospital (in which this correspondent was born) and, for the dying, a Mary Ann Evans hospice.

It's nothing more than a label, the literary civic equivalent of those mass-produced Led Zeppelin T-shirts worn by girls who wouldn't know *Houses of the Holy* if it bit them on the arse. You doubt me? The town didn't have a bookshop until 1999.

That other proponent of realism, Ken Loach, was also born there, but you wouldn't know it at all from visiting. Mind you, Mary Whitehouse was also a Nuneatonite, but I'm glad no one knows that.

Inhabitants of nearby locales refer to Nuneaton as 'Treacle Town'. The etymology is obscure, but one popular explanation is that it's because Nuneatonites are so thick. Charming, if not entirely unfair. Still, at least our accent isn't as bad as theirs. Ours is more of a watered-down Brummie. For an example, think Pete Waterman (but only briefly, please). It's not just the accent that is pitiful either. The days of mining and car manufacturing are far behind it. These days, the town is little more than a dormitory for the belt of industrial estates that surround it,

Nuneaton photos: Adam Steiner

making it something like the Little Middlesbrough That Couldn't.
Mike

LOST IT

Years ago, my friends and I used to have this game called The Alzheimer's Line. The aim was to come up with the best single thing you could say to demonstrate to your nearest and dearest that you no longer had your faculties.

The contest for the best line was won by: 'The worst mistake I ever made was leaving Nuneaton to come to art school in the Sixties.'
Linda Grant

A SEXY CORRECTION

There was a bookshop long before 1999, next door to what is now the Indian Red. It was subject of the headline 'Sex on Sale in Nuneaton' in the *Tribune* when they stocked Madonna's book, entitled *Sex*.
hullablue

NUNEATON DEFENDED!

I understand that this article is a satirical side-swipe at Nuneaton and how dreary the place is. I get it, I grew up there. However, your derision of the Capital of Disappointment jars with me. Nuneaton had a good bookshop for years in, fittingly enough for Nunny, The Arcade on Abbey Street. Imagine Acorn Antiques with more print.

I have fond memories of placing a special order for (now prepare yourself to hold your hands to your face, à la Edvard Munch) a Russian-English dictionary for my key stage three Russian course that (brace, brace) Higham Lane School provided for students in 1994. A literary wasteland? I'm not sure your labels stick. Although, admittedly, I did flee in 2000.
Russo-Nunny

'TREACLE TOWN'

Many people today assume that Nuneaton got its nickname 'Treacle Town' because of the presence of a factory producing sugary spread. But there never was one. It really is just because the town is slow and boring. Even in the 18th century, the Birmingham antiquarian William Hutton described the town as being 'in the dominion of sleep'.

CRAP TOWNS TRIVIA

COVENTRY

Motto: Camera principis (The chamber of the prince)
Population: 316,000
Average house price: £134,000
Famous residents: Lady Godiva, Peeping Tom, Philip Larkin

In earlier centuries, a favourite way of insulting people was to 'send them to Coventry'. That's to say to ignore and ostracise them so completely that they might as well be in the Midlands town – and so enduring social death. And that was before the town really started to decline.

After being totally and utterly bombed in the war (half a cathedral and one street are all that remain) Coventry was rebuilt with the 'great on paper' idea of putting a ring-road around it for ease of travel. This does provide a quick travel around the city, but, unlike the M25, it has only a couple of miles' circumference so the massive, dirty elevated road can be seen from virtually anywhere in the town centre. Yes, it makes escape easy – but for those of us who have to stay, it's a constant reminder that we're inside one of the circles of hell.

Phil Graham

MAY I COMPARE THEE TO A BAG OF SHITE?

We used to be one of the engineering and car industry capitals of the world. Now you'd be lucky if we can find a petrol station that hasn't been ram-raided. Most of our former glorious manufacturing heritage has either been demolished, or is currently on fire.

Now as you approach the town, the signpost reads: 'Welcome to Coventry – the city in Shakespeare's county'.

CRAP TOWNS TRIVIA

POETIC JUSTICE
Coventry was the birthplace of the poet Philip Larkin. The fact that he preferred to spend most of the rest of his life in Hull tells you most of what you need to know about Coventry.

Yep – that's all we've got. After hundreds of years and after countless generations have lived here, the best thing we can proclaim is that it's QUITE near to Stratford, which more than 400 years ago was the birthplace of some ruff-wearing ponce who is best known nowadays for boring the dirtboxes off our poor school kids.

If there were any justice, the sign would read: 'Welcome to Coventry – just use the pedal on the right.'

Anon

A BAD TRIP

The one and only high point of my time spent in Coventry was a rather surreal one. My housemates and I were enjoying a pleasant afternoon in an 'altered' state and decided to walk into town.

On exiting the awful subway under the ring road onto 'Ye Olde' Spon Street, we were greeted by the site of a dozen grown men

morris dancing.

We held in the rising tide of hysterics only until a pair of American tourists stopped and asked how they might get to 'Shakespeare Country'. Cue a solid 10 minutes of glee-filled laughter and stomach cramps at the fact that they were so far off track and so blissfully unaware.

Still, what a shit hole.
Stewart Whyte

PEEPING TOM

The phrase 'Peeping Tom' has its origins in Lady Godiva's legendary streak through the streets of Coventry. The aristocratic nudist undertook her ride through town in order to persuade her husband to ease the taxes on the local populace. Before she set off she requested that everyone stay indoors and cover their windows in case they caught sight of her lady parts. The grateful townspeople did – apart from Tom, who peeped through a hole in his front door, saw Godiva in all her naked glory, and was instantly struck blind.

CRAP TOWNS TRIVIA

6

GIBRALTAR

Motto: Nulli expugnabilis hosti
(No one's going to chuck us off
this rock)
Population: 30,000
Average house price: £102,000
Famous residents: John Galliano,
Barbary Apes

Yes, it's next to Spain. But it's still British.
And it's still rubbish. Even if the weather's
a bit better.

Gibraltar is a dystopian vision of what the
Mediterranean would have looked like if Britain
had conquered Europe – a strange blend of
1960s Torremolinos, Ceauşescu's Bucharest
and Bognor Regis.

UNION JACK-OFF

The Rock has been defiantly British ever since it was ceded by Spain under the Treaty of Utrecht in 1708. The result of such eager patriotism is a *Daily Express* reader's vision of paradise, from the red telephone boxes to the black-helmeted local bobbies, the sun-tanned locals' fluent English and a marked absence of euros. They even have a Marks and Spencer's. In fact, Main Street – the commercial centre – could be almost anywhere in Britain, with a parade of shops (several of which are empty) that include Burger King, Next and Morrison's.

The locals are a little too well dressed and polite to qualify as bona fide Britons, but they compensate for this with a display of Union Jacks that makes Britain look positively restrained.

Guidebooks advise crossing the border on foot from La Linea, which contains all the worst aspects of a Mexican border town – the

CRAP TOWNS TRIVIA

STAY APES
In *The Innocents Abroad,* Mark Twain wrote about Gibraltar apes and how strange it was that they weren't found in Spain. 'Of course those apes could travel around in Spain if they wanted to,' he wrote, 'and no doubt they do want to; and so, how sweet it is of them, and how self-denying, to stick to that dull rock, through thick and thin, just to back up a scientific theory.'

petty criminals, prostitutes and all-pervading stench of stale urine – without any of the redeeming features. Worst of all, because the Spanish don't like to officially acknowledge the existence of Gibraltar, they won't tell you where it is.

Things don't get any better when you manage to find Gibraltar. In an attempt to make the colony look larger than its 2.5 square miles, the local authorities have devised a labyrinthine public transport system that ensures that visitors take almost an hour to reach the top of the famous rock.

This summit is inhabited by Europe's only native apes – Barbary Macaques – who are responsible for 92 per cent of all crime in Gibraltar, stealing smartphones, handbags and cameras from unsuspecting tourists.

Surprisingly, the Spanish want Gibraltar back. Even more surprisingly, in a 2002 poll, 98.4 per cent of Gibraltarians voted to remain part of Britain. Perhaps the solution could be to cede part of Britain to Spain. How about the Isle of Sheppey? Who wouldn't welcome the opportunity to enjoy Spanish culture without having to endure the ordeal of budget airlines? The citizens of Sheppey would also probably benefit immensely from the introduction of tapas bars and flamenco dancing. They couldn't make it worse . . . Could they?
Phil Boakes

109

YORK

Motto: Let the banner of York fly high
Population: 198,000
Average house price: £214,000
Famous residents: Guy Fawkes, Ivar the Boneless (Viking Chieftan), Joseph Rowntree, Septimius Severus

When the Romans were around, York had something going for it. They made it their Northern capital, filled it with baths and other tokens of civilization and built a chuffing great wall. But then the Vikings burned the place and that was the end of that. The town has been trading on half-ruined past glories ever since.

'You've lived here ten years,' says my wife (or 'the' wife as she's known in these parts). 'How can you possibly say anything negative about York?'

The daffodils bloom brightly beneath the sweeping city walls and there are enough old buildings to keep a coachful of Americans snapping and flashing like it's a Hollywood premier, blocking the pavement whilst you try to nip to HMV during your lunch break. When it's sunny – which it sometimes is – the city is a glory to behold. But if you want to live in a postcard, I'd recommend you choose instead one of those Donald McGill creations bulging with saucy innuendo or a nice beach scene replete with golden sands and trembling palms.

York has museums galore, places of interest and many impractically narrow snickleways. Jorvik celebrates the blood-curdling brutality of the Vikings but never shows them with horns on their hats, slapping the faces of schoolboys across the globe and, particularly, the aforementioned American tourists who have, after all, come a long way and have no interest in historical accuracy. Other museums also dance on the knife edge of credibility: a Quilt Museum which makes no attempt to explain the meaning of the word 'tog' and a Museum of Early Music which makes no attempt to explain the meaning of Chris Moyles.

And then, if you have time, it's off to the tourist attraction where Guy Fawkes was probably born; the tourist attraction where W. H. Auden may have written some poems; and the tourist attraction where Judi Dench may have eaten a sandwich.

In short, the whole region has succumbed to a cheesiness that puts the wen in Wensleydale. But, when asked if it isn't all a bit touristy, the average Yorkie will doubtless answer: 'Nowt!'

This inability to give a coherent response is

quaint but they are a hardy breed defined by their razor-sharp bluntness and a pathological determination to call a spade a spade. An invaluable skill, perhaps, when your ancestors spent their working life underground foraging for lumps of coal, but less of an evolutionary advantage when it comes to maintaining the social interaction required to keep the lights on and the fluoridated water flowing.

And it's not very polite.

They are friendly, of course (to each other) and – like the rest of their Northern kin – do all the work so that we Southerners don't have to.

But the main appeal of York – well, to this Southerner – was the property prices. After all, you can buy half the Shambles for the price of a modest two-up-two-down in the South. But beware! Once you're here all the treasures in York Minster aren't enough to buy an empty box of Swan Vestas in Godalming.

And then what can you do to go home?

Nowt!

Dave Lynott

[ROVING REPORT]

I visited York twice in 2012. It was flooded both times. I returned early in 2013. It was flooded. Then I went back again. It was flooded again.

Sam

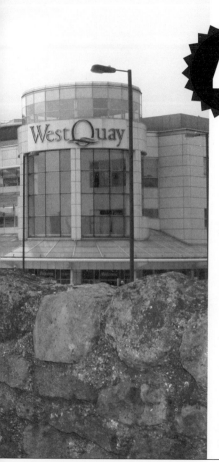

4

SOUTHAMPTON

Motto: The gateway to the world
Population: 240,000
Average house price: £177,000
Famous residents: William
Champion (the drummer from
Coldplay), Craig David (R&B crooner),
Howard Jones (1980s haircut), Ken Russell
(film genius)

The *Titanic* sailed from Southampton, and
famously, it didn't return. And since 1911 it's
been downhill all the way. Southampton was
bombed to smithereens in the war, covered
in concrete in the 1960s and overloaded with
laughably ugly shopping malls in the new
millennium.

MONOMANIA

Southampton is what happens if you take a historic industrial port city and plonk it in the south of England. Rather than planning it with some kind of civic pride, around what its inhabitants might need or want, it becomes instead a vast repository for people from the New Forest, Hampshire, Wiltshire and Sussex to buy stuff in, then piss off from. Over the last 25 years it has built one giant mall after another, each bigger and more hideous than the last, until finally WestQuay ate most of the city centre, which is now a continuous strip of chain pubs.

CRAP TOWNS TRIVIA

CRY, CRY, CRY
Southampton's current town crier glories in the name of John Melody. He can bellow 'OH YEA' at a mighty 104 decibels.

It's not all shopping and boozing, however – Soton also has a Russell Group university in the suburbs, full of Monsanto-funded snobs, which impacts the city little but for a preponderance of bars playing trip hop.

Even Southampton's councillors seldom live in the city. The port is mainly staffed by robots; the Solent is blocked off by a dozen cheap luxury flat developments.

So what do the people who grew up in the place do? They get out, if they can – and if they can't, they fight each other, in a small city that has a level of violent crime close to that of Manchester. The last time Southampton's city fathers had an idea that didn't involve building a shopping mall, it was to build a monorail. Enough said.

Owen Hatherley

THE WORLD'S BIGGEST SMALL TOWN

Take a look at a map of the UK. You see roughly in the middle of the south coast that there is an opening? Looks a bit like the country's bumhole? That'll be Southampton, the world's biggest small town, whose main claim to fame is that the *Titanic* sailed from there, killing hundreds of locals in the process.

But that was in the glory days. Now, it's a cultureless abyss with amenities and nightlife that make Chelmsford look like New York.

Southampton: the only place in the UK

[BAD COUNCIL]

CRETINOUS

In February 2011 someone going under the name of 'commnurse' joined the fray on the comments section of the *Daily Echo* website. 'It's so amusing to see that the petty-minded, bigoted, inbred of Southampton have decided to have their say on here!' she wrote. 'I only wish that the rest of you led fulfilling and worthwhile lives, but I expect in truth you do not.' She further expressed the opinion that locals were 'cretins who are quick to stand and point [and] will never realise this, get a life.'

Commnurse had a further series of bust-ups on the website, leading the *Echo* to look into her identity in September 2012. Imagine how surprised everyone was when it was revealed that 'commnurse' was actually Anthea Thorpe, wife of Asa Thorpe, a local council cabinet member.

I've ever seen someone get on a bus and nonchalantly spark up a crack pipe.
Kingnotail

TIME WARPED

Southampton is a catastrophe: decrepit, ugly old docks, large retail parks and supermarkets built right in the city centre, Soviet-style tower blocks and a plethora of abandoned shops.

It's somehow still a major cruise port, but I pity anyone who stops off here. The city has no tourist attractions to speak of (save for a piss-poor *Titanic* museum, and a towering pile of scrap metal), and it's uglier than Shane MacGowan.

For an image of 21st-century Southampton, just imagine the most awful place you can think of. But as it was in the 1980s.

Dystopian

CRAP TOWNS TRIVIA

FOOTBALL CRAZY On 23 November 1996 Ali Dia made his debut for Southampton FC. Up until a few months previously, this young man from Senegal had been an undistinguished player for the undistinguished team Blyth Spartans. His fate changed when the manager of Southampton, Graeme Souness, received a call from someone claiming to be George Weah, the Liberian international and former World Footballer of the Year. Weah told Souness to look out for Dia, and that he was a Senegalese international of outstanding talent. This call was followed by another, apparently from the legendary French international David Ginola, who persuaded Souness to sign Dia sight unseen.

So it was that Dia was substituted on to the pitch 32 minutes into a game against Leeds Utd. Dia did his best to keep out of the action and thus avoid displaying his manifest lack of skill, but before long he was left in front of an open goal – and managed to miss. Souness realised the extent of his error and called him off. It later became clear that Dia had never played for Senegal and was actually a mature student taking a course in business studies at Newcastle University.

'I don't feel I have been duped in the slightest,' said Souness afterwards. 'That's just the way the world is these days.'

Dia's manager at Blyth Spartans also refused to criticise his former player. 'At least he played in the Premiership,' he said, 'which is more than I ever did.'

CHIPPING NORTON

**Motto: We can't go on like this
Population: 6,000
Average house price: £229,000
Famous residents: Rebekah Brooks,
Jeremy Clarkson, David Cameron**

As Surbiton is to suburbia, New Orleans is to carnivals, Paris is to l'amour and Sodom and Gomorrah are to naughty sex, so is Chipping Norton to rank corruption, lurking evil and spouting on about cheese.

Those who haven't been to Chipping Norton probably imagine it as one of those beautiful Cotswold towns with solid, elegant buildings made of soft honeyed stone. They probably also think of red telephone boxes, bicycling vicars, pretty gardens and cosy pubs. They'd be right too. It gets surprisingly cold in winter, but otherwise there's a refreshing lack of concrete, and even more welcome lack of chain stores. Okay, every other building's an estate agent, but we also have lots of antique shops, boutiques, an old-fashioned hardware shop, a decent independent bookshop, not to mention a good chippy (geddit?).

So, in plenty of ways, it's a nice little town. I think I'd even enjoy living here if it weren't for one thing. Or rather, several hundred of them. You see, the trouble with Chipping Norton is that it's full of shits.

CRAP TOWNS TRIVIA

CHIPPING NORTON WHAT CLUB?
The Chipping Norton Yacht Club was established in January 2013. Its website declared it would provide: 'provide an opportunity for the Cotswolds' sailing community to get together, share experiences, hear interesting speakers, find crew, swap gear, enjoy social meetings, share a meal and exchange general "scuttlebutt" at the bar'.

Chipping Norton is more than 100 miles from the sea.

The crimes of the Chipping Norton Set are well known – but the most galling thing for me is that people here are content to let them get away with it. They like having these criminals nearby. They see the manifest corruption, the destruction of the NHS, the banjaxing of the economy, the brown-nosing of Rupert Murdoch and demonisation of anyone who earns less than £100,000 a year and think, 'I'm going to vote for them again'.

In short, it's the spiritual home of the malaise gripping the UK. If there are any other Crap Towns in the country, a good deal of the blame must lie with Chipping Norton. It is the cause and karmic repository for their faults too.

Beveridge

CHIPPING NORTON DEFENDED!

It's all very well portraying Chipping Norton as a nest of conservatism, but the town also has a rich rock and roll history. Keith Moon once owned the Crown and Cushion hotel where he held week-long parties and developed his alcoholism. 'Baker Street' was recorded in a local studio. Fairport Convention have long lived nearby. And now we are the home to the lovely and beautiful Alex James, the bassist from Blur.

Becky Millett

BLURRED VISION

Notorious cheesemong Alex James is indeed a good example of the Chipping Norton way of life: but this isn't quite so rock and roll as your correspondent Becky Millett seems to imply. He is after all someone who wasn't ashamed to be a member of the Groucho Club and proudly claimed to have blown a million quid on Champagne and cocaine. He now spends his time banging on about cheddars and pretending to be a country squire. Some of his thoughts about life in Chipping Norton recently appeared in the *Daily Mail*. The highlight was his description of taking on two 'local women' who came 'from the nearby trailer park' to clean his house. Said James: 'They fascinated me.'

And there you have it. Chipping Norton: a pretty place and a microcosm of everything that is wrong with the country, now with extra expensive cheese.

Daniel Layte

TOP GEAR (1)

Why are you laying into Alex James when Jeremy Clarkson lives in town? In fact, James should be admired for moving to Chipping Norton. In most places he'd be considered the smuggest git around. Here, he isn't even in the top ten.

Tom Humphries

CHIPPING NORTON DEFENDED AGAIN!

This is utter, lazy rubbish – Chippy is a great place to live with friendly, helpful people and a thriving, independent, mixed community – just look a little further than the obvious and the cliche of the 'Chipping Norton Set' – who of course don't live in the town but surrounding villages. True, there is a degree of suspicion of newcomers who wish to model it into green-welly-and-Barbour-hat land – but that just seems sensible to many of us. If you were to look at the town notice board outside The Fox, you would get a sense of all that goes on. Alternatively the kebab van in the centre of town is a busy place every night!

Oh Dear

TOP GEAR (2)

Some insights:

1. The locals, once you get to know them – which, granted, could take anywhere up to 12 years – are some of the nicest and most welcoming people you will ever meet. They may appear aloof, but I'm convinced it's because Chipping Norton's residents are well-practised at pretending they didn't just see the prime minister squeezing a melon, Alex James buying a roll of sellotape, or Captain Jean-Luc Picard trying to manoeuvre a super-wide vintage Jaguar into a parking space no wider than a motorbike.

2. It's the highest point in the Cotswolds (on a par with the Ural mountains in Russia) so the views are spectacular. But it's fricking freezing in winter and walking about town for any length of time will murder your shins.

3. For a tiny town in the middle of nowhere, it's remarkably well served. You can get pretty much anything you want (as long as you don't want it after 5pm or on a Sunday).

4. Unless what you want is cocaine, which you can get anywhere, any time . . .

Helen Pockett

CRAP TOWN LEXICON:

YARN BOMBING

The habit of wrapping bits of knitting around lampposts, trees and other innocent inanimate objects. Chipping Norton has been subject to a sustained campaign from an unknown midnight knitter whose creations have appeared all over town. No one knows why.

THE CHIPPING NORTON SET

The country lanes around Chipping Norton are clogged by SUVs belonging to annoyingly rich people. These include motormouth Jeremy Clarkson, Old Etonian horse-trainer turned thriller-writer Charlie Brooks, his infamous wife Rebekah, and Prime Minister David Cameron.

The Chipping Norton Set hit the headlines in summer 2011 when the *News of the World* phone-hacking scandal broke. It turned out that, as well as getting entangled in the phone-hacking scandal, Rebekah Brooks had been inviting David Cameron to her massive house for 'country suppers', lending him horses, and informing him that when he signed his text messages to her 'LOL', it meant 'laugh out loud' rather than 'lots of love'. Cameron was also a guest at a Christmas get-together at her house that included James Murdoch, chairman of News Corp, just as the media mogul was putting in a sensitive bid to take over an even greater share of BSkyB, and apparently trying to destroy the BBC.

'We would prefer to be put on the map for more positive things,' Chipping Norton mayor Chris Butterworth told the *Guardian* at the time. 'I don't really know what the Chipping Norton Set is . . . I'm sure it is just an informal thing.'

His wife Sue added: 'Surely people are allowed to have supper at Christmas with their neighbours . . . Such a lot has been made of the celebrity factor. But we have a lot of well-known people in the area, because it is a beautiful place, and people are allowed to get on with things.'

She neglected to mention that those things include tapping into other people's phones and trying to rig the UK political system.

Daylesford Organic is one of the most famous haunts of the Chipping Norton Set. It's a farm shop selling ecological, fair-trade-food-porn produce: a place where you can even get your dishwasher salts in brown paper bags, to make them look that bit more rustic and earth-friendly.

This is not your average deli. Far from it. In fact, far from everywhere. Although it aims to be local in all things, Daylesford isn't really local to anyone. It's miles from the nearest settlement, in a big field. So the only way to get hold of their environmentally friendly food is to travel there in your polluting car. Judging by the car park, you have to go there in a very big car too. Preferably a Range Rover. It was these gleaming rows of over-priced metal that first told me how unusual this place was. There was only one

car in there that was worth less than £40,000. Mine. But then, people in Daylesford have very different ideas about prices.

A friend had pre-warned me about the expense, claiming that when he'd visited he'd seen a piece of driftwood on sale for £350. Even so, I was astonished. I spent a long time turning over price tags in amazement and fear:

Tea towel: £30
Candle: £10
Olive oil, 750ml: £16
Wellies: £60
Bottle of Champagne: £100
Two garden urns: £10,500

That's right: £10,500. I noticed, because a woman had turned the label over and screamed.

'This place really isn't for me,' the woman said. I knew exactly what she meant. It was for a very different kind of person. Someone like . . . 'I've just seen Samantha Cameron buying her lunch!'

It was my better half, Elly, back from her own tour around the shop.

'Really?'

'It was definitely her. She had that nose and that long look. She was by the cheese. She saw me looking at her and she took on that awkward look celebrities have when they know they've been busted. I even felt sorry for

THEY AREN'T EVEN NEW!

her, for a minute. But then I remembered how much her lunch must have cost, compared to, say, a month's dole money, and so . . .'

By that time I'd noticed something quite alarming. Elly had a bag in her hand.

'I've just spent £50,' she said. 'But I've bought us supper.'

'For a week?'

'No.'

Later that week the papers reported that the Camerons had gone on holiday to Spain.

'Mindful of how a luxury holiday would appear amid massive public spending cuts, David and Samantha Cameron flew to Spain with budget airline Ryanair to celebrate her 40th birthday,' reported the *Daily Mail*. 'And despite their wealth, they stayed in a three-star family-run hotel.' The whole thing must have cost them less than their lunch.
Sam

BRADFORD

2

Motto: Progress, industry, humanity
Population: 294,000
Average house price: £142,000
Famous residents: Rita, Sue and Bob Too, David Hockney, Sir Henry Irving (who died on stage in Bradford)

Bradford is a city with a giant hole in its heart – literally and metaphorically. Its once great industrial strength has withered. And they've gone and dug up most of the middle of the town centre.

CRAP TOWNS UPDATE!

POSITION LAST TIME: 39
REASONS:
• Costs, Cocks, Queues.
• Even Bill Bryson disliked it. It existed to make every other town look better.
RECENT DEVELOPMENTS:
• Everything has got worse. Much worse.

Bradford photos: Eloise O'Hare

SECOND WORST

A once fine and confident Victorian city has been brought to its knees by years of truly incompetent planning and failed developer-driven attempts at 'regeneration'. If the planners and the politicians had left well alone Bradford might have survived and prospered. Might . . .

Every time a national league table is published Bradford is at the wrong end of it. Congestion, segregation, school standards, derelict land, burglaries, home repossessions, crap high streets, postal vote rigging, youth (and other) unemployment, overall deprivation, etc. You name it, we're bad at it.

We've even got the second worst schools in the country. That's right. We couldn't quite manage to be the worst; another mediocre performance from the lads at City Hall. However,

There are not many reasons for visiting the city centre nowadays. In fact it would be preferable to drive around on the inner ring road . . . If only it actually went all the way round. Yes, Bradford fails even in that.

I nearly forgot, they did finish something recently. They had a pool built next to the city hall so people can go into the centre for a paddle. Stone from China was used to build it. It cost millions of pounds. And it was just what Yorkshire needed. Another puddle!
Arfa Teacake

I understand we did manage to top the league for female genital mutilation.
Sorrow and Anger

SICK JOKE
As a former resident, revisiting poor old Bradders is like going to see an increasingly sick relative. You can still remember why you love it, but Lord it makes you sad. And smells of wee.
Ripper

CRUSHING EMPTINESS
In Bradford city centre many fine Victorian buildings have been demolished. Much of the 1960s crap that replaced them has also gone. The old department stores have all gone. Many shops have closed. Many pubs have shut. The only things that ever open round here are pound shops and charity shops.

[BAD COUNCIL]

A NEW HOPE

The Bradford Odeon is an art deco gem that, among other things, once hosted a well-known beat-combo called The Beatles for the first concert of their first UK tour. It sits in the heart of the world's first UNESCO City of Film. It's the last remaining 1930s super-cinema in the UK. It was built from local materials and with an entirely local workforce. It's also beautiful. So, of course, Bradford's local authorities have dedicated years (not to mention a small fortune) to destroying it.

Possibly the most hilarious demonstration of the authorities' refusal to listen to local opinion came in 2005 when Yorkshire First (a government quango who bought the cinema in 2003 with public money, hours before it was due to go for auction) launched a design competition to find a replacement for the cinema. They opened the final entries to a public vote. The public voted overwhelmingly for the design that kept the most of the original building. So Yorkshire First declared a completely different design the winner – one that, not coincidentally, involved knocking the cinema down.

Since then it's been a grubby story of vested interests, fingers in fishy pies and strange happenings. Pipes inside the building were cut, causing extensive water damage and strengthening the case for demolition. At one stage, the also-involved, council-allied and ironically titled Bradford Centre Regeneration (BCR) committee declared that 'virtually nothing' of the building remained apart from its 'decaying outer shell'. Urban explorers promptly entered the building and posted dozens of photographs of its surprisingly well-preserved interior.

Helpfully, the Conservative head of the local council in 2007 also declared: 'That red brick building is not some startling piece of architecture. It doesn't matter.' Locals disagreed. In 2007 thousands of them even surrounded the building in a 'hug'-based protest – but even though £25 million was spent on a fountain and some puddles just down the road, they were repeatedly told that, in order to save money, the building had to

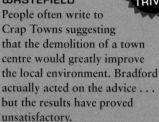

BRADFORD WASTEFIELD

People often write to Crap Towns suggesting that the demolition of a town centre would greatly improve the local environment. Bradford actually acted on the advice . . . but the results have proved unsatisfactory.

2003 Planning permission was awarded to build Bradford Westfield, a 51,000 square metre shopping centre in the middle of the town centre. Unfortunately, there was no clause about completion dates.

2004 Demolition work began, clearing a huge site and demolishing several buildings right in the middle of the city. In 2006, demolition ended.

2009 After years of inaction it was announced that plans were 'put on hold'. In 2010 nothing happened so Bradford council turned some of the site into a temporary park.

2013 A 15-acre hole remains.

go and offices built in its place.

Happily, for once, fate was kind. Yorkshire First were abolished and responsibility was handed over to the Homes and Communities Agency who, after much legal wrangling, sold the cinema back to the council for £1. It may yet survive. The tide in Bradford may finally be turning . . . There is hope, even for this currently (almost) crappest of towns.

1

LONDON

Population: 8,174, 100
Average house price: £461,000
Famous residents: The Krays, Boris Johnson, Barbara Windsor, Michael Caine, David Essex

'Hell is a city much like London,' wrote Shelley, which pretty much makes the rest of the UK a declining suburb of Satan's realm. Such is the inequality in wealth in the UK and in the focus of government policy that the 'Great Wen' controls and affects everything else in the country – and not in a good way.

CRAP TOWNS UPDATE!

POSITION LAST TIME: 17
REASONS:
• Costs, Cocks, Queues.
RECENT DEVELOPMENTS:
• Bendy buses came and went. Boris came and stayed. The Olympics made the queues even longer and the costs even higher.

THE NICE THING ABOUT LONDON IS THAT EVERYONE LOOKS SO HAPPY

London claims to be a world city – a modern, 24-hour metropolis – but this is mostly just a pretense put on for visitors. Spend an extended time in the place and you'll see that it just doesn't stand up.

Evidence of this can be seen in the mad dash for the tube on Friday and Saturday nights when the public transport system effectively shuts down shortly after midnight. This leaves revellers with the choice of being abandoned in the city centre having to dodge aggressively driven rickshaws, people illegally selling reconstituted pork cylinders of indeterminate origin or stag and hen parties from the Home Counties overexcited to be in 'big town' and therefore prone to committing random acts of violence against its inhabitants.

To get home after the tube has closed leaves people with the options of black cabs (to pay the fare you'll need to remortgage your house – oh, but I almost forgot this is London, you'll never be able to afford a house here anyway), a minicab, in which you stand a high chance of being sexually assaulted – as we're cheerily reminded each Christmas – or a night bus, which is a must for all fans of vomit, paranoid schizophrenics and R&B played through tinny mobile phone speakers.

Also, for a world city, we are spectacularly unprepared for almost any eventuality. Be it snow, rain, heat or any of the other weather conditions we get every year, the city will almost certainly grind to halt. Yes, we managed to pull off the Olympics but that was an anomaly. What the Mayor called Londoners' 'Olympic spirit' was more like stunned disbelief that for once everything seemed to be running smoothly.

There are three very important things to remember when living in London that will stand you in good stead:
1. Always stand on the right.
2. Never eat in an Aberdeen Angus Steakhouse.
3. Don't even think about speaking to somebody that you don't already know.
Patrick Dalton[6]

[6] You can find more of Patrick's view on London on ShitLondon.co.uk, along with lots of funny photos.

THE CITY OF LONDON

....

Motto: Domine dirige nos (Lord, guide us)
Average house price: £575,000
Famous residents: Dick Whittington, Dick Whittington's cat, Ronnie Kray

....

The place that helped develop the transatlantic slave trade, blew up the South Sea Bubble and gave you the banking crisis.

From Monday to Friday the City throngs with the comings and goings of various new religious sects; the bankers, brokers and traders; the soothsayers and hedgers of futures. At weekends Markets rests and the Square Mile falls largely silent, yet the City never really sleeps. Its pavements and roads are worn down from the constant visits of Politicians seeking favours from Markets, meeting with their favoured priests sometimes called Cronies, or examining the answers to their prayers known as Holdings or Dividends. And should any politician's faith lapse, even if only for a moment, the City sends out its evangelists, called Lobbyists, who remind them of the power and will of Markets.

For years the City called upon the people to give up their old ways of manufacturing

CRAP TOWNS TRIVIA

DICK-ISH

Legend has it that Dick Whittington was a poor boy who turned up in the City of London with nothing more than his cat and a dream. Thanks to his willingness to try, try and try again, he rose to become Lord Mayor, a living embodiment of the virtues of meritocracy.

But the truth is that Whittington, like almost everyone else in the City of London, didn't earn his wealth. He was born rich and stayed that way, feeding off the rest of the city like ebola on your insides. He didn't even have a cat.

GETTING MEDIEVAL

'It seems to be that every big trading disaster happens in London, and I would like to know why,' asked Congresswoman Carolyn Maloney in the US House of Representatives in 2012.

It's mainly the fault of the city's electoral system, which works on principles abandoned in the rest of the UK in the 1830s because as a review at the time declared, they 'neither possess nor deserve the confidence or respect of Your Majesty's subjects'.

There are 25 electoral wards in the Square Mile. Four are given to residents. The remaining 21 are divided up between companies in the City, based on their number of employees. Not that workers actually get to vote. Company bosses appoint selected voters to 'represent' them.

and producing in favour of services. All was well for a while and the people thrived. But the doctrine of light-regulation was abused by the priests of the City, who indulged in sins of miss-selling, rate-rigging and money-laundering. Markets was displeased and brought down twin plagues of debt and deficit. The priests called on the people for sacrifices known as bail-outs, and the Politicians decreed an age of fasting and Austerity to appease Markets. And a great darkness fell over the land – though the City still thrives.

Paul Emmanuelli

Meanwhile, there are four layers of elected representatives in the Corporation: common councilmen, aldermen, sheriffs and the Lord Mayor. Want to stand? No problem, become a freeman of the City of London. And in order to do that you have to be approved by the aldermen – generally by becoming a member of one of the City livery companies. Want to become a member of one of those? Or even know what they are? How's your medieval history?

At which point, I'm guessing you are confused, which seems to be the plan. Everything about the organization is opaque and bewildering. It's near impossible to find out how much money it controls, how much property it owns, how much power it wields.

We do at least know that it has its own private police force and better still its own militia. It also has someone called the Remembrancer, who gets to sit, unelected, in the House of Commons, right behind the Speaker's chair and check through all legislation that the House passes.

On top of this weird influence, an investigation by the Bureau of Investigative Journalism recently uncovered a £10 million lobbying campaign by the Corporation to defend the financial sector. Yes, that does mean the people who got us into the never-ending post-2007 recession in the first place. And yes, the local government of the City, which isn't properly elected, lobbies for a sector that acts contrary to the interests of the rest of the UK.

CRAP TOWNS TRIVIA

CROYDON
PICTURE SPECIAL!

CRAP TOWNS UPDATE!

POSITIONS LAST TIME: 32 and 15
REASONS:
• Violence, malaise, despair.
• Floor littered with KFC bones like an ancient caveman dwelling.
RECENT DEVELOPMENTS:
• In 2012 Croydon council applied for city status, promoting the borough's many historical virtues in a document called Croydon: The Facts. One 'fact' was that, among 50 other celebrities, the poet Lord Byron was 'born locally' and was one of 'many talents nurtured by Croydon'.

A problem soon emerged. Byron was born in Marylebone and never visited Croydon.

Paul Sowan, vice president of the Croydon Natural History and Scientific Society, said: 'The people who researched this didn't even bother to check with their archives service, which could have saved a lot of embarrassment.'

Billboard photos: Naomi Adams

TOTTENHAM

Motto: Audere est facere
(To dare is to do)
Average house price:
£240,000
Famous residents: Lemar,
Adele, Bernie Winters

If anything, Tottenham's probably too easy a target, what with the riots still being pretty fresh in the memory and it hardly being known for being a charming old place to live. But then, surely that's the problem?

As soon as you hop off the tube, or train, or bus, or any other of Tottenham's sole selling points (its range of escape routes) you get the same feeling everyone gets on arriving: you are not welcome here.

It's hard to pinpoint it exactly. The pavement looks like it was bought to function as a death trap, slab

fragments pointing accusatively from the ground at mad angles. Probably pointing at the people who have hawked all the saliva in their bodies onto them. Or the ones who used them as open-plan bins for their betting slips. Or maybe they're showing where all those sinister and half-finished trails of crimson drips around the place actually lead.

There are plenty of reasons why you might be in a bad mood in Tottenham. Even including the bleak and dystopian retail park, there's so little money to be made here. So little work. And there are just as few places where you want to spend money. Or even your time. No cinema. No high street shops. The first and last time I went to watch the football in a pub, all I ended up watching was the racism of the white regulars and landlord.

So it's no wonder the place seethes with such barely restrained violence. I saw two kids innocently kicking a ball past – not even into – an abandoned car showroom get stopped by a police van packed with six officers and grilled before being ushered the way they were going anyway. I saw one driver just drop another in the road with a single punch after one nudged into the other's car. I even saw some drunken arse gracelessly scale the gates of the middle-class fortress that is the gated housing complex one night, right in sight of the biggest police station in north London, and no one saw fit to do anything about it (and thank God they didn't, I'd had far too much punch to explain I'd left my gate fob somewhere in Finchley). At least the mayor of London is doing something about all the ill will felt towards the heavy-handed and ever-nervous police here: he's cutting the station's hours from 24/7 to 40 a week.

People will inevitably, and lazily, blame Tottenham's crapness on its sheer range of disparate groups, gangs, communities and congregations. But all those people do have one thing in common: a total lack of hope that Tottenham will ever change. While we're still there, the rest of the city having written off the place as a confusing mess of differences beyond reform-by-gentrification, we shuffle mean-faced, dodging the spit and bones on the pavement, making for one of those myriad escape routes, at least for the day.
James Elliott

MAYFAIR

Average house price: £3 million
**Famous residents: The Duke of Westminster,
Russian criminals**

Its inhabitants are, virtually without exception, the biggest shower of needy, self-important bumwipes in London, with a self-pity complex and misplaced sense of entitlement to match. The architecture is either dull West London stucco or a twattish approach at some kind of meaningful landmark building. Either way, it's rubbish. Most importantly, the pubs are shit. And full of people who live in Mayfair.
Seb OB

TEDDINGTON

Average house price:
£700,000
Famous residents; **Benny Hill, Noel Coward, Andi Peters, Julian Clary**

CLASS BORE

I grew up in Teddington. In those days the people were a mixture of working and lower middle class – anyone with money lived in Richmond and Kew. A few streets were so rough that the policemen were said to walk in pairs for safety.

I remember when the first genuinely middle class people moved into our road and – to my parents' horror – they didn't have carpets or net curtains ('You can see right in!').

By the time I moved out, in my early twenties, almost everyone I'd grown up with had disappeared, houses were being restored with their original Victorian features and shiny new cars lined the streets. The last time I went to Teddington – a year ago – it felt completely soulless and, yes, I saw some of those awful mothers. I'm not sure Teddington is a town any more, as it seamlessly merges into Hampton, Twickenham and Kingston, but it is a very dreary, overpriced suburb.
Steerforth

GLUM

Steerforth, you're absolutely right. I've been living in Teddington for 22 years and now it's stuffed to the gunwales with corporate middle-managers with their fertile wives who appear unable to get to Starbucks without the aid of a 4x4.

Given the dosh these fools pay for a Victorian semi with rising damp it's no wonder there's not a single decent restaurant around here. I presume most of hubby's salary goes on servicing the mortgage and the school trips for the their overweened little darlings.

No wonder all the married blokes look so bloody glum around here. Did they really leave the throb of bachelordom in Clapham for all this? Shame.
Fred White

APPENDIX: NOT SO CRAP TOWNS

When we started getting tweets and messages encouraging us to produce another book of Crap Towns, almost as many missives came in challenging us to 'find something nice to say, for a change'. Including from my own mum. So we thought we better do it. Our original intention was to produce a top ten of the most improved former Crap Towns. But we soon discovered that most had become far worse. Ten was too much of a stretch. Even so – and in spite of the current economic climate – we did manage to find five that had bucked the trend and become better. They deserve all the praise they can get. Heck, you might even want to visit them. Might . . .

Sam

NOT SO CRAP
HULL

Motto: The gateway to Europe
Population: 250,000
Average house price: £133,000
Famous residents: John Prescott, Peter Mandelson, Philip Larkin

CRAP TOWN UPDATE
POSITIONS LAST TIME:
1 and 19
REASONS:
• Smelt of death.
• The local council blew a fortune on daft schemes such as building £40 million stadium for Hull football club, and fitting huge numbers of empty council houses with new windows shortly before they were scheduled for demolition.
• Poo found in phone boxes.
RECENT DEVELOPMENTS:
Hull no longer smells of death. The chocolate factory that

caused the city's notorious pong has closed. The subsequent job losses have taken away some of the sweetness – but at least the local air is now breathable.

Elsewhere, there are similar stories of one step forwards and another backwards. Hull won a lot of regeneration cash in the boom years, but since the recession many schemes have been stopped mid-way. Many have fallen through.

But at least the city hasn't got much worse. And considering the last century of rapid decline in Hull, this lack of downward movement might be considered an improvement. It's now possible to hope that the town has finally hit rock bottom. There are promising new projects like the huge World Trade Centre Hull & Humber and a prospective wind energy machine manufacturing plant, suggesting Hull is regaining some of its spirit of trade and industry. It's still one of the cheapest places in the country to buy a house. And as Philip Larkin famously said, it remains 'nice and flat for cycling'.

Sam

NOT SO CRAP
BEDFORD

Motto: Pride in Bedford
Population: 153,000
Average house price: £220,000
Famous residents:
Eddie 'The Eagle' Edwards, Terry 'The Prisoner' Waite, Wolf People

CRAP TOWN UPDATE
POSITION LAST TIME: 33
REASONS:

● A representative from Bedford's twin-town Bamberg was murdered in a hotel foyer.

● The Queen visited. The council repaved the side of the street she walked along. But not the other.

● Locals regard a visit to Milton Keynes as a treat.

RECENT DEVELOPMENTS:
Undaunted by its lack of coastline, Bedford has developed the popular Bedford by the Sea festival, when sand is dumped in the town centre, funfair rides are erected, and Punch and Judy shows are performed. Lots of people seem to really enjoy it.

Crap Towns HQ have also received dozens of emails demonstrating that Bedford is is a haven for eccentrics, misfits and people who leave their teeth lying around:

It was at the end of October 2012 that I was waiting in the hell-hole that is named Bedford Bus Station when something ever so peculiar caught my gaze. This discovery didn't even surprise me, knowing what I know about the standards of some of the Bedfordians. **Amy**

An old man in Bedford bus station once came up to me, hooted like an owl and ran away flapping his arms. **Will Porter**

A man with a suit and briefcase used to stand outside Woolworths for hours meowing.
Wolf People

It's actually starting to sound quite interesting . . .

THE SOCIETY

Joanna Southcott was an 18th-century prophet who died in unfortunate circumstances. She had told her large public that she was pregnant with the next Messiah. Instead of giving birth, however, she died. She had actually been carrying around a large cancerous growth.

But she did leave something: a box which she said contained the secret of eternal bliss. It came with the instructions that it wasn't to be opened until a time of great crisis – and only then in the presence of no fewer than 24 bishops of the Church of England. However, that didn't stop the antiquarian researcher Harry Price taking a look. In 1927 he staged a public opening. The contents included a horse pistol, a lottery ticket, a dice box, a purse, some old books and, most enigmatically, a nightcap.

The story didn't end there. Soon after Price's exhibition, an ex-lunatic-asylum patient called Mabel Barltrop came forward to say that Price had opened the wrong box and that she had the original. What's more, pretty soon Jesus Christ was going to come along and establish the New Jerusalem near her home . . . in Bedford.

Barltrop gathered together quite a following, known as the Panacea Society. They proved expert at raising capital and soon started buying properties around Bedford in readiness for the day when Christ came to take up residence. They also took out newspaper adverts requesting that bishops came forward and opened the box.

Unfortunately, the box remained closed. The society kept its houses ready and waiting for Jesus to move in until shortly after the turn of the millennium. For a long time, their biggest dilemma was whether to install a shower – since they didn't know whether Christ would have a radiant body and therefore not need conventional plumbing. But when He hadn't shown up by 2004, the two surviving members turned the society's assets over to the management of a charitable trust. They set up a permanent exhibition in one of the houses. It's now open. It is weird – and wonderful.

Liverpool photo: John Block

NOT SO CRAP
LIVERPOOL

....

Motto: Deus nobius haec otia fecit (God gave us this unemployment)
Population: 466,000
Average house price: £163,000
Famous residents: John, Paul, George, Ringo

....

CRAP TOWN UPDATE
POSITION LAST TIME: 7
REASONS:
- Full of monuments to uselessness, like St John's Beacon – a daft tower that glowed pink during a local radio station's 'love hour'.
- Excess sentimentality.
- Violence.

RECENT DEVELOPMENTS:
Suggesting that crap is as much state of mind as architecture and economics, Liverpool has transformed itself from one of the nation's most maligned to most loved cities in the last ten years.

Its architectural wonders were recognised by UNESCO in 2004 and granted world heritage status. It put on an incredible show as European capital of culture in 2008. Cruise ships have started to pull right into the heart of the city thanks to its new cruise liner terminal . . . As one correspondent to Crap Towns put it, the city has stopped navel-gazing and started looking seawards again.

On a smaller scale, the local council has started pioneering headline-grabbing regeneration schemes such as offering derelict homes for sale for £1 to those who will fix them and live in them. The city has also developed a thriving arts and culture blogging scene. And yes, I know that last sentence made you want to puke, so let me prove it. Here's sevenstreets.com on the worst restaurant in Liverpool:

'The chef here is world class. He's amazing,' purrs our waiter as he brings a bottle of house white (thin and tasteless. Like Victoria Beckham's anorexic pret-a-porter collection. It was both 'free' and 'overpriced' at the same time.) . . . The Prego Pollo Fritto – chicken in breadcrumbs with barbecue sauce – honestly made you re-evaluate Ronald McDonald's place on the culinary map of the city. These bullets of gristle were burned, dry and unyielding – in another century they'd be used as lead shots in muskets. Although, sadly, we fear they'll do more damage ingested. Two hours later and I can still feel my stomach pleading with my colon to take them off its hands.'

Poetry! Sheer poetry!

All those jokes about tracksuits, moustaches and thieving are starting to seem terribly out of date.

Sam

CRAP TOWNS TRIVIA

GRACELESS

Astonishingly for a former Crap Town, in 2004 Liverpool turned down the opportunity to destroy its skyline. There was a plan to build a 'fourth grace' to overshadow the beauty of the Three Graces: the Royal Liver Building, the Cunard Building and the Port of Liverpool Building. Locals reacted in horror, writing thousands of letters to planning authorities, and soon the public sector money was withdrawn.

Sadly, the council have been trying to spoil things since, by giving planning permission for Liverpool Waters, a giant set of tall buildings and flats that may be built right next to the Three Graces. UNESCO have put the area on its world heritage status danger list and English Heritage have warned of 'adverse impacts'. It might all be about to go tits up again. Although, as defenders of the scheme point out, where else in the UK are developers thinking of investing so much money?

NOT SO CRAP
MORECAMBE

··

Motto: Beauty surrounds, health abounds
Population: 38,000
Average house price: £130,000
Famous residents: Mr Blobby, Eric Morecambe, Thora Hird

··

CRAP TOWN UPDATE
POSITION LAST TIME: 3
REASONS:

• People used to poo on the steps of the Midland Hotel.
• Looked like the setting for a Morrissey song.

RECENT DEVELOPMENTS:

Morecambe hit the headlines when 20 Chinese workers digging for cockles met tragic deaths in the bay's treacherous quicksand, exposing the terrible conditions too many in the area have to endure. Noel Edmonds also appeared in local papers saying that he feels 'sorry' for the people of Morecambe because the local council have had to include a levy on their council tax to pay him back the £2 million they owed him after a disastrous attempt to build a 'Crinkly Bottom' theme park. Nothing was said about whether the tidy-bearded entertainer intended to give any of the money back.

But in spite of such troubles, Morecambe has turned a corner. The Midland Hotel, until recently used as a large al fresco toilet, has been repaired and looks gorgeous. It alone is worth a trip to the seaside town. Admittedly, that visit will still have the feeling of pioneer tourism. There are more boarded shops than almost anywhere else in the country – which is saying something. But there are other gems in town. Locals have lovingly restored the glorious winter gardens building, the long prom with its incredible views over the Lake District hills has been spruced up. There's even a decent local band at last, The Heartbreaks. And they don't sing about every day being like Sunday, they sing about Morecambe being fun. Visit on a sunny day, and you'll believe them.

Sam

NOT SO CRAP
HACKNEY

....

Motto: Justia turris
nostra (We have a
righteous tower)
Population: 247,000
Average house
price: £470,000
Famous residents: Eli Hall
(who staged the longest
house siege in UK history),
Iain Sinclair

....

CRAP TOWN UPDATE
POSITIONS LAST TIME: 10
and 12
REASONS:
• Council's anti-corruption
department investigated for
corruption.
• Reported burglaries per
1,000 of population 11 times
the national average.
• Local accident and
emergency ward pronounced
worse than Soweto.
• Local MP Brian Sedgemore
was mugged. The assailants
made away with a bag of chips.

RECENT DEVELOPMENTS
Hackney has attracted a vitriol usually
reserved for Tory politicians and paedophiles.
Until lately, the area was famed for warring
estates and knife crime, but now Hackney
is widely perceived as embodying the worst
aspects of gentrification. Vintage boutiques,
French-style cafés and pop-up art galleries
adorn the streets, and you are never more
than six feet away from a babyccino. Nowhere
are Britain's ever-rising levels of inequality
more evidently pronounced.

The big problem is that house prices in
Hackney and the rest of London are going

up faster than Chris Moyles chasing a pie. This is pricing out the locals, but compared to similar areas, Hackney is still relatively cheap. This means that young professionals who can no longer afford the inner city have been moving in en masse, with their university degrees and penchant for artisan sourdough loaves. Friction with the local working class population is inevitable.

On the one hand, in Hackney you are confronted with some of the worst poverty in the UK. It is no longer 'murder mile': the levels of serious crime are much lower than they were a few years ago. However, the murders, suicides, muggings and gang-related bust-ups continue on a daily basis. Schizophrenia and delusional disorders are five times the national average, the rate of people citing mental health conditions for being unable to work is amongst the highest in the country, and thousands of children go to school hungry. Hackney also recently came top in the national 'cuts per person' league: £266.17 from 2010/11 to 2012/13: four times as much as the rest of the UK.

On the other hand, everywhere you turn there are graphic designers with too much, too silly facial hair and girls dressed up like pin-ups from the 1950s, sipping soya lattes while loudly extolling the benefits of a plant-based diet, and talking about the latest independent film they've been working on. In Dalston, pissed-up hipsters have been causing friction by taking dumps in local residents' gardens. Everyone is either working, or trying to work in 'the media'. They would all define themselves as 'creative' and they are all trying really hard not to be the girl in 'Common People'.

And even if you are lucky enough to be one of these trendsters, chances are you will be so enveloped in clouds of self-hatred and middle-class guilt that you won't be enjoying your privilege half as much as you should be.

Your bus journey home is just as likely to be disturbed by a stabbing, a local religious fanatic informing you that you will go to hell because of drinking, smoking and pre-marital sex, or by a jaded yuppie sitting behind you, trying to convince their friends that they 'deserve' the right to do huge amounts of cocaine every weekend, because they work so hard.

Ultimately, the transport is slow, the rent isn't actually all that cheap, and everyone is sick to death of talking about the perils of gentrification. But Hackney these days is too much of an easy target: the parks are beautiful, the area's history is incredibly rich, it's one of the most culturally diverse boroughs in the country and, at the moment, there is nowhere I would rather live.

Kathryn Bigelow

AN ELEVATING STORY

When I lived in a new-build block of flats in Dalston, someone took to relieving themselves in the lift. I moved back to southeast London. Far more civilised. (Apart from the time a crack addict took a shit in the alley outside my house.)

Riptari

Hackney photos: Kathryn Bigelow

town hall

INDEX

First published in Great Britain in 2013 by Quercus Editions Ltd
55 Baker Street, Seventh Floor, South Block, London W1U 8EW

A CIP catalogue record for this book is available from the British Library

HB ISBN 978 1 84866 222 3
EBOOK ISBN 978 1 84866 223 0

10 9 8 7 6 5 4 3 2 1

Designed and typeset by Liz Edwards

Printed and bound in China